CRIME, COMEDY & COMBAT

William Clegg

First published in Northern Ireland in 2020
by Excalibur Press

ISBN: 978-1-910728-58-1

Formatting & layout by
Excalibur Press

Cover design
Oranga Creative

Excalibur Press
Belfast, Northern Ireland

team@excaliburpress.co.uk
07982628911 | @ExcaliburPress

excaliburpress.co.uk

"The most precious thing we have is our memories."

William Clegg 2020

CONTENTS

FOREWARD

The Way We Were – about the author

My name is Paul Graham and I, like the author, was a child born in the 1950's and grew up in the Bangor area in the 1960's and 70's. My first awareness of "Willie" Clegg was this mad daredevil who was in the year above mine at Bangor Grammar School. I recall him pulling a 150 yard wheelie along College Avenue in front of the old school on his BSA Bantam with an audience of maybe a hundred admiring schoolboys in our blazers and skull caps. He was older than me, taller than me and clearly quite a bit cooler than my greasy adolescent persona. He was one of the cool kids. But not in a bad way. With his mop of hair and flashing smile, I seem to recall he was a pleasant character, unlike some of the older boys who treated their juniors with disdain. The great teenage feat that Willie was known for in those years was the ride along the sea wall at Queens Parade. In those days we still had a beach on the seaward side and the potential fall of thirty feet riding along eroded stone slabs less than two feet wide, was truly a death-defying stunt. He had assistance to lift the bike onto the wall at one end and off at the other and did it for a bet. These kinds of feats had him as somewhat of a local legend in those heady days, the early days of the Northern Ireland "Troubles".

Years passed and I joined the RUC in January of 1977. Without going into my full bio, I had many of the same or similar adventures as Willie and in many of the same far flung corners of our province, just not at the same time. On days off, Bangor was a place to relax, unwind and have a social life. It was in that arena in the late 70's and early 80's that I found myself drinking in the company of Willie and others who were likewise young and full of vigour and shared experiences. He was still a couple of inches taller than me and he had a great air of charm and confidence. We became regular drinking buddies for a few years and graced the bars of Bangor with our presence along with a few select mutual friends. Often when the bars emptied, we would drift back to Willie's house where the parties were a regular event. Of course, he had his beloved black Ford Escort RS2000, the hot car of that time. I once took it airborne from the railway bridge on Crawfordsburn Road, while on an errand to get more cans of Coke from the vending machine at Bangor RUC Station. I landed safely though! Time progressed and I got married and started raising a family. I still bumped into Willie in the pubs of Bangor but as I was trying to stay married, I had to stop going to the parties at Willie's house. No social media or even mobile phones back then to stay in touch. At one point when Willie was Station Sergeant in Carrickmore he invited me to transfer down there and we could finally have the pleasure of working together, making loads of money with the massive overtime. I slept on the idea and decided against it, because at the time I was stationed in Bangor and I couldn't get the image out of my head of my funeral and fellow officers commenting, "What a feking moron! Stationed in Bangor and volunteers for Carrickmore and gets killed!" Also, my girls were young and it was good to be home every night for their sake.

We remained on friendly terms and bumped into each other from time to time at Jenny Watts, or Fealty's enjoying manly drinking time and swapping stories, probably some of those in this book. The last I heard of Willie was when he retired from the Police (now PSNI) and was still unmarried. Did I mention that Willie was something of a lady's man, as well as a man's man? He still had his passion for motorcycles and adventure and my last memory was that he was heading off to

Thailand to be a Scuba diving instructor. I moved to the USA in 2007 and it was only via the power of Facebook that we got reacquainted. So, I wish him the best recording his collection of memories about his time in the force, and hope that you enjoy his musings as much as I did.

Paul Graham 12662 Detective (retired)

NOTE FROM THE AUTHOR

These recollections, reflections or stories were originally written for my son, William Moore Clegg, who made all things worthwhile. I wrote them before they were forgotten because he was not born until I was almost 50 years of age. They do not need to be read in any particular order.

Although loosely following a timeframe, I have placed them in accordance with the 11 subsection titles. They have been, only slightly, amended from my original scribblings for personal reasons. I hope you enjoy them almost as much as I have in writing them.

"A word is not the same with one writer as with another. One tears it from his guts, the other pulls it out of his overcoat pocket."

Charles Peguy, The Honest People

William Clegg
2020

PREFACE

Sorrow and Beauty

"All the world is a stage and all the men and women merely players, they have their exits and their entrances; and one man in his time plays many parts".

Just like the old soldiers who fade away, most morphed into themselves as naturally as seasons becoming more solitary and resolute behind facades of time and tides. Showing less of themselves to a world which occasionally needed them, had also cruelly battered, worn, aged, though prepared them for what might lie ahead. They had echoed laughter and sorrow, tragedy and comedy, joy and mourning through experiences which were perhaps more than just character forming. Most became hardened, more detached from emotions by measures of stoicism, cynicism and dark humour. A cocktail of calls and scenes attended their true souls now only familiar to themselves. The parallel histories between police barracks and policemen of old, their existence and demise inextricably linked. A new era dawned almost a generation ago, and another and another and another.

If there is a book you really want to read but it hasn't been written yet, you must write it!

W.J.T. Clegg 13219

PROLOGUE

THE PROVINCE

'There's no place like home'

George Best, Samuel Beckett, Blair Maine, Barry McGuigan, Seamus Heaney, Rory McIlroy, C S Lewis, Oscar Wild, Liam Neeson, Flann O'Brien, Joey Dunlop, Alec Higgins, Dennis Taylor, James Nesbitt, Carl Frampson, William McKee Strong, Sir Kenneth Brannagh, Michelle Fairley, Bronagh Gallagher, Stephen Rea, Amanda Burton, Adrian Dunbar, Jamie Dornan, Freddie Gilroy, Van Morrison, Paul McEvoy, Gary Moore, AP McCoy, Mary Peters, Wayne McCullough, James Ellis, Percy French, St Patrick, Francis Tomelty, Eddie Irvine and of course that famous Denizen Bob Catterson.

Of course Northern Ireland is also famous for many features such as but not exclusive to the Titanic, The Giant's Causeway (although once described by Samuel Johnston the compiler of he first English dictionary as worth seeing but not worth going to see) it is still an impressive sight, the Sunderland flying boat which flew from Castle Archdale in County Fermanagh to locate the Bismarck during the Second World War.

Whether we Northerners refer to ourselves abroad or at home as 'Ulstermen' or 'Irish men' or whatever the occasion merits, there is no denying that the island of Ireland both North and South has spawned plenty of talent and geniuses, especially when one looks at the tiny little spec it barely displays on an atlas of the planet.

During the last 20 years I have travelled extensively from

Ecuador to East Java, from Scotland to Sumatra and from Comber to Cuba meeting and finding out about different countries, races religions and traditions. However, I have never met any people more interesting, colourful and personable than those from Erin's green isle.

Before these travels and more locally I served the public whilst in the Royal Ulster Constabulary during the 70's 80's and 90's and in the dark period known as 'The Troubles'.

In total I was stationed in 15 different postings throughout the length and breadth of the 6 countries.

(The actual province of Ulster includes three other counties which remained, by consent, in Eire – those of Donegal, Cavan, Monaghan. Interestingly and in true Irish fashion Donegal, in the South of Ireland, is geographically more northerly than the North!!!).

During that time, I became familiar with every city, town, village, and 'Huck' of a place in Northern Ireland (and also quite by error whilst on duty one in the South).

The diversity and dichotomy here in the North seem to ebb into some obscurity almost exponentially with the increase of distance from it. Surely then to most we are 'Irish' in the way that everyone on the Emerald Isle was Irish before the creation of the six counties 1921? And yet, curiously on our beloved home soil differences of identity and culture paradoxically return.

I love my wee country. I love the fact that every county has its own accent or dialect peculiar to the location. The only exception as far as I may distinguish are folk from the East coasts of counties Down and Antrim, due I suggest to their closeness in proximity to the West Coast of Scotland.

I am always glad to feel the jolt upon landing followed by "Ladies and gentlemen welcome to Belfast (or Dublin) International Airport".

Each of our six counties is different in one way or another; County Down has it's rolling drumlins, Strangford Lough and the Mourne Mountains. Antrim has the Giant's Causeway with its basalt volcanic hexagonal blocks, valleys and nine glens. Fermanagh has its lakes, islands and waterways. Tyrone has the stunning vistas along the length of the Clogher Valley and beautiful Cookstown, home of the family sausages and the widest main street in Europe. Armagh for the seat of the ancients of Ireland and its orchards and County Londonderry has its rolling beach coastline, historic maiden city along with undulating vowels and consonants.

Sometimes when I return home to roost from travels abroad the odd soul may say "I don't know what you are doing back here". That's a little sad I think for although I love to travel and experience new thoughts and feelings I know where my 'Blue Bird of Paradise' nests.

After all, to be happy at home is the ultimate result of all ambition.

ITCHY FEET

"Go West Young Man"

There wasn't much to do in the 1930's for a youth growing up in an isolated part of County Down. I suppose that's why my father read a lot. He attended Regent House Grammar School, of which his parents were very proud. His father had collected many historical and literary books ranging from Shakespeare and the classics to Charles Dickens, Castles History of Ireland, as well as popular period novels. Notably the works of Oscar Wilde would have been an athema then and were not included.

In the 1960's every Sunday (after Sunday School and Church), when I wasn't allowed out to play (or if I hand been 'grounded' during the week for some misdemeanour), I could take my comic and sit in the 'good room', as it was called then, at the front of the house. Our rented 1950's style red brick semi-detached house was in suburban Bangor. These treasures broke the monotony of no television and the torture of Mario Lanza or 100 Best Classical Tunes played on the dansette record player.

I vividly recall that 'good room', which always smelt of the new, plain yellow ocre carpet combined with the turf burned smell, the ashes of which remained in the grate of the open tiled fireplace. There was also the musty smell of old books and the piano that sat in there, purely to fill the room and give it more character. We were so seldom in there; except at Christmas time or when someone special like, the Reverend Burke, called to spread some word or the other.

I now have of all these books in a bookcase, which I made in woodwork, at home. I tell my son that these are a 'fountain of knowledge' and maybe someday he will pick little pearls and pieces out of them, as I did. On the prefix of one of these books it read that "Fear in danger is 10,000 times more terrifying than danger itself" (Daniel Dafoe).

I remember my mother telling me a simple line of verse, 'Of all the sweetness ever sent, there's none so sweet as sentiment", It was 1962, I was at home with my mother while both my elder sisters were at school and my father at work. I was 4 years old.

In my own cottage I have accumulated, over the years, hundreds of old photographs, most are kept in a biscuit tin – the lid on which is depicted a scene shown from an elevated position of Trafalgar Square in London, the black Austins, Humbers and Vauxhall cars would indicate the year to be around 1950.

Some of these photos are sepia, some black and white, a few are in colour. Most are loose, others are bound in bundles embraced with pretty ribbons of pink and blue silk with the elegant bow on the front.

These have been left to my custody by my parents and grandparents. A few have the year written in pencil or water-ink on the back. A fewer have names or even places noted. All these people are now merely ghosts, other faces familiar to some other phantoms being washed away like tears in rain.

A few of the latter ones are familiar to me only because me or my family are present. Here at Westport with my sisters and my grandfather who died when I was only 7. There the famous Elden Hotel in Skibbereen, family trips taken in Ford Corsairs and Morris Oxfords.

So, what becomes of other people's memories…? Must they vanish with the sands of time? The humour, the agony, the ecstasy, the joy? Are they all doomed to a nothingness?

On all my own photos I have noted the year, names and places as far as I can remember, so much in the future for my own benefit as anyone else's should they be interested. Now when I look at the black and white photographs of my Training Squad dated 19th March 1978; every face evokes a memory. Many now gone by deeds fair and foul. Some souls march on.

These ramblings and reflections were initially jotted down for the benefit of my son who is almost 50 years younger than me. They mushroomed from thoughts I had whilst walking, scuba diving and motorcycle riding, always alone. They became my playthings.

I hope the reader enjoys these novellas. They are not designed to be just a catalogue of events nor parables, nor metaphors and neither do I wish to provoke murmurings of "Well he would say that wouldn't he?"

There's a wonderful opening line at the beginning of one of my favourite movies which goes as follows: -
'Ever since I can remember, I always wanted to be a gangster'
– Ray Liotta Goodfellas 1990.
Me? I never dreamed I would be a cop! My wage at Crazy Prices (a local supermarket) then was £35 per week, my first pay slip in the Training Centre shows £162 per month, so it wasn't about the money.

Image: Me in the Summer 1977

I always had a part-time job whilst at school, enough (with help from my mum and dad) to buy a second-hand Triumph Bonneville in maroon and white colours. I used this to act out my hero – Marlon Brando in 'The Wild Ones' – as I posed and pouted my way around, complete with leather biker jacket and engineer boots which I still have to this day.

I was working as a Trainee Manager in Crazy Prices whose tag was 'We Chop the Lot'. This included any workers found slacking. I was also studying Maths and Physics in the local college. It was there I met a great friend Tom, a youth about 2 years younger than I was who was in the Royal Ulster Constabulary (RUC) Police Cadets at the time. (This was a precursor to the regular force and recruited young people from 16 – 18 years of age). I knew both he and his older brother whose family had moved to Bangor town under terrorist threat to their father who was a serving officer in the

RUC at that time. His brother Brian, Ciaran, Cary and I were part of 'The Dudes' every Sunday night in the local carpark.

1977 saw Mark 1 and Mark II RS2000's Ford Cortinas in various guises, Datsuns, Minis, Mazdas and Toyota Celicas gleaming under the shimmering neon car park lights. Many were family cars on loan, the premise being good exam results.

It was young Tom and another more wayward friend of mine Johnty who encouraged me to apply for the RUC.

I had met Johnty and Frank about 7 years earlier when they had 'borrowed' my Raleigh chopper – but that story is for another day!!

I applied in December, sat with the interview board in January and arrived in Enniskillen Training Centre on 19th March 1978. I had just turned 20.

TRAINING 1978

'Then a soldier, full of strange oaths... and bearded like a pard'

Jealous in honour,
Sudden and quick in quarrel
Seeking the bubble reputations even in the cannon's mouth'

EARLY YEARS

"Then a Soldier full of strange oaths and bearded like the pard jealous in honour, sudden and quick in quarrel seeking the bubble reputation even in the cannon's mouth".
Shakespeare - As You Like It

In 1978 the road system in Northern Ireland was sparse. Only 2 motorways left from Belfast; the M1 to Dungannon and the M2 to Antrim. The RUC Training Centre was then situated in Enniskillen in the County of Fermanagh, a total of 40 miles to the South West via Dungannon, then approximately another 50 miles via towns, villages and 'A' class roads to the destination. The drive at that time took me around 3 hours.

Fermanagh is a beautiful border county framed by counties Donegal, Leitrim, Cavan and Monaghan in the Republic of Ireland and County Tyrone in the North. Its heart is the town of Enniskillen situated almost entirely on an island between Upper and Lower Lough Erne.

In all it is picture-card perfect and is famous for its hospitality, fishing and rain!!

My clothes on arrival in a Mk II 1600E Cortina were equally fashionable... Biker jacket and boots, faded Levis, shoulder length hair hiding the customary earrings which I had forgotten to remove. A cross between Alvin Stardust and Sid Vicious!

The armoured 4m tall gates mostly concealed the interior together with an ominous blast wall encircling the entire complex. This wall was crowned with a 3metre diamond patterned chicken wire fence to prevent objects being thrown over. As I got out from the car, a pair of slate grey eyes showed through the viewing slot, provoking thoughts of an illegal gambling joint in USA. 'Sniper coloured eyes' I immediately thought as I remembered a short story I had read in English literature; when the rest of the class dutifully read 'Greek myths and legends' as assigned. "Yes?" they questioned, "Recruit" I volunteered, "Go away" they flashed as the portal clunked shut.

I rapped the iron gate again. It still sounded like tapping the hull of the Titanic. To my right 4 eyes now peered at me from the security box adjacent. "Your papers, where are your papers?" One pair queried and glanced furtively at the grey eyes beside them. He sounded like one of the German soldiers in 'The Great Escape'. "In the motor" I volunteered. "Produce them" he barked. I did and a mechanical clunk was heard, entry was sanctioned, no way out, I thought of Colditz!

Upon admission a 3 storey Victorian building paraded itself behind a small patch of manicured lawn to the fore of which was a drill square instantly recognisable by three smooth parallel lines etched on the tarmac by decades of marching parade boots. The whole visage screamed of discipline. A new era beckoned.

Training voraciously devoured 14 weeks which would require another volume of anecdotes. I was fascinated by the numerous characters from all walks of life.

The 'Squad' consisted of a wide spectrum of recruits ranging from Civil Servants, Accountants, ex-Army personnel, University Graduates (qualified, failed and non-committal), school leavers, previous full time Reserves and Police Cadets, Doctors, Lawyers and 'Indian Chiefs' (I just made that up!).

One memorable incident comes to mind.... First thing every morning before breakfast was forming up and marching from the rear of the building to the parade square for inspection by the Drill Sergeant.

One morning we were standing and filed in order waiting for the order. Suddenly a message for the Drill Instructor. Off he marched, his highly bulled/polished job/nailed boots glistening from above and sparkling from the hobnails on soles as he went. How long for? Ours was not to question why...

We remained frozen in time with the crisp Spring air around us. Alarmingly as we stood like clay soldiers in a cavern, a voice somewhere to my right whispered in my ear, "Willie, you forgot to shave mate!" "Fuck" says I. Options flashed across my mind, run for the shaver or run away?! How much time did I have – moments, seconds, none? Bathroom or Back squaded'? Could I even move? Automatism!

Automatism! Now there's a word and a half. We had heard about this phenomenon in class some weeks earlier and it struck me like an electric shock which had me sent bounding outwards and upwards through the doorway in front to halfway up the linoleum covered stairway leading towards the 3rd floor, my shaving razor and the bathroom sink. All I thought I could hear was a collective "Nooooooooooooo..." receding behind me. Onwards and upwards I sped 3 steps at a time slowly slightly only on each return to skid 180 degrees across the landings. At last the summit!!

My room – there the shaving bag – there the razor. Shaving foam? Forget about it. About turn, 4 strides would have me in the washroom opposite. No time. Dry shave, no water, soap or mirror. Six of the best. Left side, right side left, 2 on the chin and 2 on the upper lip. No time to replace the razor in the wash bag – ditch the bugger on the Junior Squad's landing on way down. Heart pounding, palms sweating, feet barely touching the stairs – control the descent by skilful grip on the bannister. Forage cap in right hand. "They'll give you a medal for this should you pull it off". The final approach. The exit to the outward doorway widened with the mouths of my Squad mates beyond and there the gap where I had once stood. Controlled skid into position as before.

Then... nothing. Not a breath nor a murmur. Eyes front – where was the Sergeant?? I froze but my eyes remained scanning. Still nothing but something was wrong, what was it?? As my dust settled the Drill Sergeant appeared from my right. Then the orders... "Squad shun. Right turn. Link-right, link-right, link-right..." My instincts told me, along with the feelings of desolation, isolation and barrenness that I was doomed! My marching movements were in auto pilot, I had an 'out of body' experience telling me I didn't want to be there. He knew, this wily old Coyote missing nothing.

Stationary and with blood pumping around my ears I was dead in the water but somehow although I had been cast adrift, I was still afloat. Why did I feel a calmness around me?? A warmth, even?? I knew it was too early in the morning for the tickling sensation on my chin to be a fly; a cut?!

I thought the scrutiny more intense than before. I felt the power of 140 eyes on me but only the 2 in front seared like those lasers in the James Bond film. Then like an exocet missile the 64-million-dollar question tore the silence asunder. "Did you shave today laddie?" "Yes Sergeant". Pause in freeze-frame. "Well next time stand a little closer to the razor" in his strong highland regimental pitch.

Six weeks of further training preceded the passing out Parade in Enniskillen in June, then my first posting. I had made it!

No3 Special Patrol Group, Belfast - July 1978

'For Peace We Serve'

I was allocated to number 3 Unit of the Special Patrol Group in Belfast, then also known as 'The Blues'.

The SPG had evolved over the years as a result of the civil unrest in Northern Ireland in the late sixties. There were 6 Units based in the Belfast area with another 4 County Units throughout the province. Our duties involved public order and anti-terrorist operations, security protection, searches, prisoner escorts and regular training exercises.

Each Unit comprised of 1 x Inspector, 5 Sergeants and approximately 24 men. In Belfast 90% of all our work was performed in long wheelbase land rovers although unmarked police cars were also used on occasions.

It was a balmy early afternoon around the end of June 1978 in Strandtown, East Belfast, when I first saw my base. It had been built in the garden of what was once a majestic detached Victorian mansion in the heart of East Belfast. The house now served as the local area police station. Our base, this bunker, was just that. More like a place to live during a nuclear explosion. Built in the 2nd world war by the occupants of the house, to serve as a safe haven, during the Luftwaffe bombing attacks on Belfast and in particular the H&W Shipyard. The 2 massive Shipyard cranes (Samson & Goliath) visible on the horizon, were probably only 5 kms as the crow flies. My mother was living in Ranfurly Drive, just up the Holywood Road when Lucy Weir's house across the suburban terrace from No 7 received an unexpected evening delivery. Luckily it was defused.

I was finishing off the driving course and was due to begin duties soon. The 'Bunker' consisted of a toilet area upon entrance, then divided into 3 distinct and separate cubes, each approximately 5m x 7m. Although the area at the rear, divided into 2 separate areas housed the section Inspector and Station Sergent's office, it was serviced by a long passageway. All internal and external walls were probably 1m thick and of solid construction. Each section had a couple of post box windows about half a metre below the ceiling, a recent addition. The second area was the designated recreation area. The sight which greeted me upon entering the recreation room was one which I would see hundreds of times over the next 20 years. Soft, low lounge chairs with tubular frames supporting a soft base and tall reclined back, the bases were, more often than not, split and sagging showing the yellowing foam base. There were three rows each comprising 4 of these seats, all uniformly directed towards a wooden effect Bush TV on the shelf about 1.5m up and of course the official dart board.

There was no daytime television in those years, so the 4 uniformed and armed police officers were talking amongst themselves whilst studiously examining the BBC2 testcard with the young girl and the clown displaced between conversations. I was wearing a blazer, brown trousers and brogues. Eight eyes spun 90 degrees and clocked me suspiciously. I swallowed hard and asked where I might find the officer in charge. A face, now familiar and friendly stated, "Just go down the back and ask for 'Nat'. I thanked them and noticed as I advanced, they all got up as to leave. "Must be end of lunch break", I thought.

Through the next area which served as the briefing Room and into the bowels of this structure, a pair of broad shoulders split with white full head of hair was writing something. He reminded me of "- . -" the morse code signal for the letter K. This distinguished gent with bushy sidelocks dressed in a shirt then looked up from the desk between us, although 50 plus, he looked like a prop forward in a rugby team.

"Nat about?" I asked. He whipped off his gold rimmed spectacles and queried "Who the fuck are you?" I knew immediately that he was to be treated with caution. His piercing look would have cut coal. "I'm Willie Clegg, a new recruit attached to this station next week. Apparently, Nat can fill me in". He spat out "You got that right son". He sprang up and rushed out of the office towards the direction of the recreation room and exclaimed "Think they're fucking smart".

This was my first introduction to Station Sergeant Pendleton, 6303 and Belfast Special Patrol Group, I was to love it!

DIVISIONAL MOBILE SUPPORT UNIT

'Once more Unto the Breach'
Shakespeare - Henry V

In as much as Dundonald, my second posting after the customary one year in the SPG, was the epitome of mundane to me, Fermanagh Divisional Mobile Support Unit (DMSU) was the Holy Grail of proactive policing in the province.

As a result of being caught for a professional indiscretion whilst attached to Dundonald Police Station, I formally requested to be transferred to Co Fermanagh and the promise of something more exciting and rewarding in terms of personal fulfilment.

Each police Divisional area in Northern Ireland had formed its own DMSU upon the disbandment of the old Special Patrol Groups which in turn was due to the public outcry on the mainland after the death of a civilian, Blair Peach in suspicious circumstances and allegedly by members of the English SPG Group.

There were 6 DMSU Units attached to the greater Belfast area which patrolled in armoured land rovers. However, in rural areas the MSU Units primarily patrolled in unmarked police cars due to the continual landmine terrorist threat.

The duties of these MSU's primarily involved public order control, protection to off duty members of the security forces and civilians via proactive policing methods, including under emergency legislation stopping and searching of vehicle and private premises, area searches for arms/munitions and assisting normal police patrol duties as and when required.

They were trained regularly in these areas and specialist 'anti ambush manoeuvres'. This proved invaluable on many occasions.

Image: Foot patrol, Thompson's Bridge, Kinawley

Note: I'm the one with the sketchpad, indicating topography of culverts in Fermanagh area

Heroes & Villains

"I have hundreds of such memories and from time to time one of them detaches itself from the mass and starts tormenting me. I feel that if I write it down, I'll get rid of it"
Dostoyevsky

SPG No3 - Strange Bedfellows

In those years and in Belfast, the Provisional Irish Republican Army (PIRA) was divided into 4 'Battalions' thus Twinbrook/Andersonstown, Ballymurphy/Lower Falls, Ardoyne/New Lodge, Short Strand – Markets. This was in accordance with their respective geographical locations.

It was a bitterly cold overcast autumn day in Belfast as we patrolled the Antrim Road area in our Land Rover. I was seated in the rear with the 2 rear gunners. We had committed to memory the vehicle registration numbers of known protestant and catholic persons of interest in the greater Belfast area. The rear doors in non-armoured vehicles were always left open in order to facilitate swift dismounting of the vehicle and to increase our vision.

Suddenly I saw a carnival red Mark 3 Ford Cortina registration mark MOI 1*05, a top suspect, MM was driving. This person and vehicle were well known to us and of great interest. I informed the Sergeant and signalled for him to stop behind us, which was permitted under the Prevention of Terrorist Act Northern Ireland.

The 2 riflemen sprung upwards and outwards to provide

cover to us as we were adjacent to the top of the New Lodge Road, well known for sniper attacks on the security forces. I alighted from the rear of the Land Rover and approached Mr M's vehicle and asked him to switch off his engine. It was my intention to search him for arms and munitions. He produced his driving documents, which were perfectly in order. The driver of our Land Rover searched the inside of the car whilst I asked him to open the boot. Whilst M and I stood at the rear of the open boot, I observed some bags which transpired to be groceries. "Doing a bit of shopping M?" I asked politely. He replied in an equally friendly manner, "Yes, just down to St George's Market". I also saw some training shoes, shorts and a running vest. "…. And a bit of training too?" I said, "Yes I have to try and keep the weight off". Then a pivotal moment, from behind the privacy of the raised boot lid I looked at him straight in his sky-blue eyes which were emphasised by a pair of gold rimmed rectangular lenses. "Do you hate me M?" Holding my stare, he candidly replied, "No, son, of course not. The country has to have a police force, it's just that ….", "Have you taken out the spare wheel?" asked Constable S. The moment had passed.

About a year later and with my time completed in the SPG I had been transferred to another police station on the outskirts of Belfast. Part of our overtime duties involved escorting prisoners from the Crumlin Road Gaol via an underground tunnel beneath the Crumlin Road to the Courthouse opposite. This was to renew the detention time by the Court for prisoners pending a trial date in the gaol. These prisoners were taken across in blocks of eight, handcuffed to each other by several Police and Prison Officers. In effect, they were merely being moved securely from one holding cell in the gaol across to another in the court and after a brief hearing, back again to the gaol.

Other officers and I had just returned a batch of 8 from the court holding area to the gaol where they were uncuffed. We have all felt instinctively that another person is looking at us out of our sight and this happened to me in the holding area at the gaol. I spontaneously glanced over my left shoulder and my eyes immediately connected with those pale blue eyes which were harboured behind the gold rimmed spectacle frames I had seen once before. The connection seemed to last an eternity.

I saw his pale pink and thin lips widen just a smidgen. Was it a sneer or a smile? But the eyes never lie.

STRANDTOWN, BELFAST C.1982

"O Villain, Villain, Smiling, Damned Villain"
Shakespeare - Hamlet

I saw him on many occasions, especially in the Ballyhackamore area of East Belfast in the Strandtown police area. We had nodded and spoken to each other exchanging platitudes on several occasions whilst I was on beat, foot and patrol duties. He was a slight white-haired individual who was probably in his sixties. He always wore a full-length Gabardine type coat which fell to below the knees. He was always alone.

I used to call into the shops in the busy commercial district which was bisected by the main road taking the mostly commuter traffic by ebb and flow to and from Belfast centre. In 1982 it was considered reasonably 'safe' for police and public. It was then and now a religiously 'mixed' area. A splendid Catholic church there by the roadside and a catholic school nearby.

As I was talking to an established shopkeeper one wet and windy winter's morning, this little figure passed by outside. "Sticky" he muttered. (Sticky is local jargon for anyone who was alleged to be or have been a member of the old 'Official' Irish Republican Army whose aims were to obtain a United Ireland in the late 1950's by violent attacks on what was known as the 'Border Campaign!').

I raised an eyebrow, "Really?", I thought. "He was in the RAF during the war but everyone in the area knows about his political leanings", he said. "Up to him", I thought – but I knew the relevance of local knowledge, i.e. that which a resident of an area automatically acquires.

I noted his comment. 2 years later (6 March 1984) I was the local Sergeant in the Co Fermanagh border police station of Rosslea. That morning I had been out on a joint police and army foot patrol in the area, around midday we returned to the joint police and army post. The newscaster on the BBC news announced that William McConnell, A Deputy Governor of the Northern Ireland Prison Service had been shot dead outside his home at the rear of the Northern Ireland Assembly Building (Stormont) in East Belfast. I became more curious as I knew exactly where he lived as it was in the Strandtown police area. This is a white collar upper/middle class area where any crime was unusual. The PIRA claimed responsibility.

Days later a man, his wife and daughter were arrested and taken in for questioning.

Eventually the 2 females were released. The man pleaded guilty in court to being implicit in the murder of William McConnell and was sentenced to gaol.

That man's name was Owen Connelly. The same innocuous little white-haired man in the long coat often seen in the Ballyhackamore shops area about a mile from the scene of the shooting. His wife Margaret admitted washing the wigs the 2 killers had used as disguises; his daughter Carmel admitting knowing her house was being used for a sinister purpose. They were moved to a secret address known only to police.

INCIDENT ROSSLEA - SUMMER 1981

"The Wheel Is Come Full Circle"
Shakespeare - King Lear

The year of 1981 in Northern Ireland was to be particularly tough for everyone. The quest for political status by prisoners in the Maze/Long Kesh prison escalated by those in the republican movement. A short hunger strike commenced in 1980 for some of these prisoners although it did not last for long. However, 1981 saw the escalation of detainees in the prison resuming this protest with further determination. Some of these men were already on a 'no wash/on the blanket' protest and up to 10 of them began consecutively over several weeks to refuse all meals offered to them sustaining themselves only with water. They continually smeared their own excretia on the walls of their cells in an effort to be treated as political rather than criminal prisoners.

Street violence and sporadic rioting was prevalent all across the North but especially in the main cities of Londonderry and Belfast. The local elections for Fermanagh and South Tyrone had been held and the seat in the House of Commons (though never availed of) was won by a narrow majority for the first time by a Sinn Fein representative who was also held in the prison and was refusing food or prison clothing. This man's name was Bobby Sands who was a convicted terrorist from Belfast. The only other party contesting this election was Ken McGuinness representing the Official Unionist.

Controversially, neither the Democratic Unionist Party representing mainly protestants, nor the Social and Democratic Labour Party, primarily representing catholics fielded candidates in this marginal constituency thus leaving the populist only 2 choices. The victory of the Sinn Fein candidate would highlight the plight of the republican movement to the rest of the world and particularly America, where there was (and still is today) a lot of support for the 'Irish Cause'.

The relevance of these foregoing paragraphs is merely to reiterate the escalation of tensions and accordingly violence all over the province of Northern Ireland, particularly the region of Fermanagh/South Tyrone at that time.

The village of Rosslea is South East County Fermanagh and lies on the border with Co Monaghan in the Republic of Ireland. It is situated 26 miles from Enniskillen in a South Easterly direction. The next closest police station to the one is Rosslea is Lisnaskea which lies roughly halfway between Enniskillen and Rosslea.

It was on a beautiful, warm, still and quiet Sunday morning in July and the Unit were resting at our base outside Enniskillen. We suddenly received an emergency radio transmission from our HQ in Enniskillen to make our way immediately in the direction of the townland of Mullaglass on the Lisnaskea side and adjacent to Rosslea village.

I was detailed to drive the first vehicle conveying a Sergeant and other Constables to the scene. I selected a Datsun 180b unmarked police car as I knew it was reliable and fast. The journey, I was later told, took just over 19 minutes to the incident point.

Upon arrival at the entrance to the scene one uniformed member of the British Army directed us to a narrow laneway on the left-hand side of the road. I had taken the most direct road via Lisnaskea and Donagh Village as we had been told the area had been made safe to travel by vehicle on route.

We arrived first. The rough stone laneway with grass up its centre opened to the front yard of a typical Irish whitewashed stone cottage complete with thatched roof.

The site which greeted us will never leave my mind.

To the yard at the front of this picturesque Irish cottage, lay four figures on their stomachs dressed in civilian work clothes. They were uniformly tied with their hands and wrists around their backs; these in turn were attached to their ankles which were raised from their knees in a skyward position. They were bounded in plastic 'zip ties' which were broader than usual and ensured these four people were rendered incapable of movement.

Only one heavily camouflaged soldier without a beret was visible. His colleagues were either out of view or had been airlifted away from the scene. He stood behind and over the 4 prisoners and faced us. He was of average height with a close-cropped haircut. His facial features were dominated by a large Mexican type moustache growing out and falling to under his chin to a broad veiny neck.

He was armed with a semi-automatic pistol which was minimised by a heavily modified and camouflage M16 assault rifle with a torch on top and a launching tube to below the barrel which was held against his hip by his right hand and pointing skywards. He also wore a broad belt containing extra magazines and other pouches of indeterminable contents. His face was covered in a random collage of green, brown and black stripes and only the movement of his eyes enabled me to make contact with them.

It was only when he slightly nodded his head and blink, did I feel the urge to get out of the police car. Here 4 yards in front of me was displayed an IRA active service unit from Monaghan led by a certain Seamus McIlwaine of some notoriety.

Between the area of these 4 terrorists and the front door of the cottage laid 3 randomly scattered and abandoned Military Assault Rifles, 2 Kalashnikov AK47's with wooden stocks and butts and a plain black standard American Army issue type Armalite rifle. Dotted around this scene were a series of other military hardware. Over there I spied 2 curved Kalashnikov magazines facing in opposite directions and joined in the middle by a ribbon of dark green insulating tape and then another 2 magazines belonging to the Armalite joined in a similar fashion. The whole scene to me was totally surreal and as of a dream.

I remember this frozen frame vividly, the warm summer breeze and slight rustling from the leaves of the trees above were complimented momentarily by the song of a blackbird on the roof of the cottage to my right and accompanied to my left by my grim looking Sergeant across the roof of the car. The tingling tremors of tension were momentarily punctuated by my Sergeant breaking wind. It sounded as though he had stood on a bullfrog!

Further to this incident and subsequent to it when we were back at base later that day, we were duly informed that a second attack had been planned on that day on Security Forces. Had the first incident been accomplished by the terrorists, a second follow up attack had been planned to blow up by landmine, the first security response vehicle, us!. This consisted of a large landmine bomb on our approach to the scene from Lisnaskea to be detonated as the police car drove over it.

I am not in a position to comment on this.

The 4 Provisional IRA men were arrested and taken in for questioning and subsequently sentenced after court for imprisonment.

The formal complaint against police made by Mr McIlwaine alleging that a police officer who was at the scene had said "That's a tasty looking piece of dirt you're eating Seamus", though thoroughly investigated, was never proved.

Seamus McIlwaine was one of 38 prisoners who succeeded in escaping from the Maze prison in 1983. He was not captured but was subsequently shot dead by Security Forces a couple of years later whilst on active service with the PIRA and waiting to attack Security Forces.

Another PIRA member was wounded in the same incident, not ½ a mile from where we had arrested him in 1981.

BELFAST 1983

Strandtown, the Last Post

Towards the end of my time in Strandtown I moved sections. He said it was due to redistribution of experience. I knew it was because we were having so much fun (especially 3 of us!) I didn't mind as I had an unofficial meeting with Chief Inspector H in the recreation room which was a one of 6 temporary porta cabins in the carpark where he rarely visited.

I remember I was engrossed, playing the 'Donkey King'/Mario video machine with Gusto – (no not another Police Officer!) when he asked me to sit down. He looked displaced in there with me. Some of the officers entered and immediately left when they saw us chatting on comfy chairs with the arse falling out of them!! I always liked this man, he was a straight talker, as were all the senior officers I gelled with on reflection.

The promotion boards were due, my 3 years of transgression were over. It was 1983. He told me to keep my nose clean and I should be fine. He was the officer writing on my file.

It was another day I was the Station Duty Officer (SDO) in the enquiry office. He entered without uttering a word and surveyed the rota on the wall of all officers attached to Strandtown. He scrutinised all the names and declared "I see there's 2 Smiths now in this barrack, aye and 2 Jones' too but there is only one King" Excellent!

But before we moved on there are some other characters who must be mentioned.

Firstly "this King" The Senior Constable commanded respect as much perhaps as any other officer I had the good fortune to meet. A broad stocky presence always immaculate in dress. Probably about 40 then and everything he did seemed effortless. He was always in good humour even when not if you follow.....

Originally from Co Antrim he had served in Hilltown (or Rathfriland) in the 60's. He told many great yarns. One was of when he worked in the earlier posting. There were 2 Constables who didn't see eye to eye, not only because one had a slight squint. One morning these 2 Constables crossed paths, one going into the Police Station and the other leaving. Neither would give way. They collided and the first man said, "Why don't you look where you're going", the other replied "Why don't you go where you are looking".

Jimmy was another senior figure in Strandtown. He had been there for some years, but it was several weeks before I actually was aware, he was attached to us. That's why they called him 'The Ghost'.

He was a fascinating almost mystical senior Constable whom everyone spoke of with reverence and appeared (or didn't!) to do whatever suited! He shared one or two of his secrets with me. My favourite was whenever he left the station on foot patrol, (always on his own), he looked for a 'defective' radio awaiting repair and labelled 'receiving but not transmitting'. He removed the label and signed it out. Then if anyone called him, he couldn't acknowledge them preferring to either go to a public telephone (no cell phones in those days) or wander back to base. I obviously asked what if he was in trouble? He gave me a glance and said, "Not likely to happen where I go cub!"

He told me that he had been great friends with an Inspector

in Firearms Branch. They had been through training together and this man had represented the RUC at Bisley in the UK mainland as a crack shot. He continued that they hadn't met for some years until his friend called at home to see him unexpectedly. They talked for a while, his friend then left and a week later this off-duty Inspector was in a shopping area in North Belfast when he happened upon an armed robbery in progress. The robber had his handgun pointed at a cashier demanding the contents of the till. The friend drew his personal protection weapon and as witnesses testified, issued the formal order – "Halt, drop the weapon, armed police". The gunman turned around in a swift action fired his weapon and shot the Inspector dead. It was a tragic incident 'The Ghost' ruminated.

He thought it extremely poignant afterwards as he believed it was as he described, "A last visit".

Between December 1982 – January 1983 I can't remember the exact date; I was on a day off and at home. Around lunch time a knock came to the front door. There stood Brian my pal from the carpark days. He had joined the full time Reserve Police a year or so before and was on his way to Co. Down border station for duty. He was excited as he was studying for the entrance exam to the regular RUC.

"Great to see ya mate", he shouted and gave me a hug "Kettle on?". We sat and drank tea that afternoon and reminisced of days gone by. About 3 o'clock I wished him a safe journey to work, we hugged, shook hands and bid bye-bye.

On 6th January 1983 he and Sergeant Eric Brown were shot dead on duty by the PIRA in Rostrevor, Co Down. Another officer who was injured in the same attack managed to return fire to the fleeing IRA members despite also being seriously wounded.

CAST A COLD EYE

W.B. Yeats

NEWRY & BESSBROOK - APRIL 1979

"We are born astride of the grave, the light gleams for an instant and it is night once more". Samuel Beckett - Waiting for Godot

Although technically a 'large town', the 'city' of Newry was founded in 1144 AD alongside a Cistercian monastery and is one of Ireland's oldest towns.

Between the two Jacobite rebellions of 1715 and 1745, this 'Gap of the North' grew as a market town situated four miles from the border with the Republic of Ireland, 34 miles from Belfast and some 12 miles from Newcastle, Co. Down which itself is seated on the coastline and at the foothills of the six peaks of the famous Mourne Mountains often romanticised in song, verse and painting by a well-known Co. Roscommon Irishman, Percy French, amongst others.

The city's name is the English version from the Irish 'An Luraigh' derived from 'An Lurach', which means 'Grove of Yew Trees'. This itself is derived from the myth that St Patrick, our patron saint, planted the first yew trees there around the 5th Century AD – (presumably whilst taking time off from rearing the swine on Slemish Mountain in Co Antrim, outside Ballymena).

There is evidence of human settlement there as far back as the bronze age.

Geographically it lies on the south-eastern part of Northern Ireland. Interesting to note is that the western half of the city lies in County Armagh and its eastern half in County Down. The two sections being split conveniently by the Clanrye River.

The entire area is based in a valley between the Mourne Mountains to the east and the Ring of Gullion to the west. It is designated as an 'area of outstanding natural beauty'. Three miles to the north west of Newry and just inside the area infamously know as 'Bandit Country' of South Armagh, nestles the picturesque village of Bessbrook of some 2,500 inhabitants.

Famed for a linen mill, founded by Elizabeth (Bess) Nicholson and husband Joseph. The 'Brook' part is a stream on its periphery. It was designed by the Quaker John Richardson – its formation probably based on the plan of the Quaker Malcolmson family town in Portlaw, Co Wexford in The Republic of Ireland and its successor is probably 'Bournville' company town outside of Birmingham on the UK Mainland, which it pre-dates by almost half a century.

The village is often depicted in illustrations to include The Craigmore Viaduct, built from granite stone mined from hillsides nearby and completed in 1851. This magnificent structure boasts 18 archways of 20 metres in height, over a total span of 500 metres and for a while it was the longest bridge in Ireland. It notably still supports the Belfast to Dublin Railway. Despite violent actions by outsiders, the village of Bessbrook was always vaunted as being one of the few areas where Anglicans, Methodists, Presbyterians and Roman Catholics abided in harmony.

Who could have imagined such an idyllic hamlet would evolve into a strategic military zone and garrison in the latter part of the 20th Century and contrary to the three Quaker tenets of no police station (nor needing one) due to the other two of no pubs or pawnbrokers (this was their PPP ideal).

Surely those 'founding fathers' might turn in their graves at the statistics of twenty-five soldiers and locals (all protestant males) being taken in the prime of their lives? (Albeit four dying in military aircraft accidents).

In April 1979, Constable Noel Webb was working in the Newry and Bessbrook area, in uniform, beat and patrol duties. I knew him well as we had completed our initial training together from March until June 1978 in Enniskillen Training Centre.

He was a quiet soul who was like by everyone. As he was around 10 years older than most of us, he was regarded as perhaps an older brother, or young uncle. Because, in your late teens and early twenties, 10 years means a lot. I remember he had an aversion to weapons. In those early months only 9mm walther pistols and antiquated 9mm sterling sub machine guns were deployed for protection by police in training on the indoor firing ranges at Connswater in Belfast and Sprucefield in Lisburn. He handled both of these as anyone else would a black mamba or water-moccasin snake!

I knew the area in which he worked was dangerous. The special patrol group I was attached to had been involved in a large-scale search operation the summer previous following a gun attack by the P.I.R.A. on two RUC officers while on mobile patrol. One officer, 32-year-old Hugh McConnell had been shot dead at the scene, the other, 42-year-old William Turbitt had been wounded, subsequently kidnapped and taken away for 'questioning'. His remains were finally discovered later in July 1979. It is believed (or hoped) he died shortly after the ambush.

Worthy of note is that the City of Newry, or town as it was then, was the scene for the highest number of deaths in one single IRA attack when on February 28th, 1985 nine police officers were killed and thirty-seven others were injured. Amongst the dead was another personal friend of mine from training days in Enniskillen, Rosemary McGuckin who was only 27.

Around midday on 18th April 1979, whilst on patrol in the Belfast area, our entire unit was tasked to go immediately to a briefing in Newry as a result of an incident which occurred the evening before. We were to perform a search of the area. We drove there and then out to the scene. It occurred on the main road between Newry and Bessbrook.

I will never forget the sight that greeted us at the scene of that incident.

On 17th April, the provisional IRA had parked a transit van containing an estimated 1000 lb of explosives at the side of the main road between Newry and Bessbrook. At around 8pm a police armoured land-rover carrying Constable Paul Gray (25), Constable Robert Lockhart (44), Constable Richard Baird (28) and my squad mate, Constable Noel Webb (30) drew parallel with this van and around a metre from it the bomb inside was detonated by remote control from about half a mile away.

The vehicle was split asunder, the only visible remains were the chassis and some of the armoured plating panels. The four occupants had in effect been vaporised by the explosion. They wouldn't have heard or felt a thing.

Our duty was to complete and resume a search of the cordoned off area of the attack. We had all been trained for incidents such as this but nothing could prepare us, or anyone, for the emotional shock. After searching all day until twilight the largest identifiable portions we found were a steel rim about 100m away and a black boot with part of a foot and leg still inside.

It was truly horrific.

For me the incident was made even more poignant (if that were possible) by the fact that I knew both Constable Webb and Constable Baird.

After dusk we drove back to our base in Belfast, not one word was spoken on the journey. Each person was left with his own thoughts and prayers, all observing an informal one-hour moment of silence, as it were. The British army presence in Bessbrook was finally removed from the area when the last troops left Bessbrook Mill on the 25th June 2007.

"The day thy gave us Lord, is ended".

No3 SPG Bomb Incident - University Avenue 1978

"When Men Were Men"
Anon

In the 70's and 80's the PIRA perfected the use of 'grill bombs' these contained smaller amounts of commercial explosives attached to incendiary mixtures and attached to the grills of commercial properties placed there to prevent burglaries or stones and rocks.

One Autumn evening in the Belfast area of University Avenue and University Road, we received the message to go to a suspect device.

The Victorian terraced houses opposite were occupied by private tenants.   Once we had closed the junction with Ormeau Road the task to vacate the residents on the opposite side was left to Constable S and myself. We went to the houses nearest and opposite the identified device hanging high on the window grill. Constable S at the first home and myself at the second. Upon ensuring that these 2 houses were safely evacuated we returned to the footpath to alert the next 2 homes when the bomb exploded. I didn't have time to do anything.

The blinding flash told me something had happened. Then there was a loud bang followed immediately by a huge vacuum drawing you towards the site of the explosion, then instantly propelling you away.

Constable S was blown into the small hedge at the front of the house he had just visited. I was blown to the ground. I was disoriented and confused, ears numb and ringing. My first reaction was to try and get up, but I couldn't. My balance was gone.

After some moments we both managed to stagger up, fortunately neither he nor I were seriously injured and no one else had been injured. The building opposite was ablaze.

Once the Fire Brigade arrived and managed to control the fire, saving buildings on either side from being affected all the key holders to the remainder of the commercial properties were called and attended. Numerous windows were broken, and I had seen a lot more damage caused by car bombs, scenes we had already attended prior to, during and after they had exploded.

When we finished work and returned to base later, still feeling rather delicate, ears still ringing and the medication was brought out – beers, spirits and wine.

We both returned to our work for the next shift that day. This was also the rule in those years unless seriously and obviously injured. No one went 'sick' and those who might have were labelled 'chocolate fire guards'. Besides there was so much happening every shift you were scared of missing something. Nowadays I'm not so sure!!

CARRICKMORE POLICE STATION, CO TYRONE 1985

'Cast a cold eye on the life, on death, horseman pass by'
Epitaph, W.B. Yeats, Sligo

On the 21st December 1985, as usual there was a big threat on in Carrickmore. Pretty much the norm, to tell you the truth. Every day there was two routes cleared in and out for cars, if need be, to travel on the road because during the hours of daylight they didn't do any mobile support or any mobile patrols at all because of the risk of land mines and attack to all foot patrols.

There was about 200 combined army and police personnel searching the Carrickmore area to allow patrols and manpower to get in and out. Every morning the police cleared two routes out of Carrickmore so there was an alternative route if they were being observed by terrorists at one.

There were only three routes in; one from Creggan; one from Drumnakilly and one from Sixmilecross. There was another one from Pomeroy but that was another divisional area.

We had information that there was going to be a mortar attack on the station, so the whole place was swamped by police from about 5.30am. The whole of the immediate and village area was searched, they were at it all day and there was only a skeleton crew left at the station. Normally there would have been two patrol sections but because of the threat; there was only me and eight other officers.

There was plenty of accommodation at the station, but it was all portacabins and if a mortar hit them it was like a match to balsawood. It would just split up. There were no mortar-proof bunkers in those days. These were introduced after the killing of nine officers in the Newry area in 1985 when they finally made fall-out shelters or mortar-proof bunkers in most of the rural stations.

Image: Single mortar attack, Carrickmore January 1986 (my room)

After searching all day, nothing was found. At about 5pm it was getting dark and the whole convoy headed back to Omagh. Half an hour later I was in one of the portacabins and thought I'd just nip out to the toilet. I was in the toilet when I heard this almighty bang. It wasn't as if I had never heard the accidental discharge, of a firearm before, and my first thoughts were that some of the boys had let off a round. Seconds later there was a large thump, followed by a blinding flash.

Suddenly all the air is taken out of the room, it went completely black. In a split second I had been both drawn into the vacuum of the seat of the explosion, then immediately spat out. This Mk10 mortar had landed about 5 or 6 yards away and gone off. The lights went out, my lights went out; then I got up, piss and shit all over the place. I really thought it was my last movement. Luckily, although I was disorientated, I wasn't very badly hurt. At least, not physically. I went back into the communications room to call in the attack, then it went quiet apart from the resounding ringing in my head, my ears were numb. In the distance I heard myself telling the radio operator to call in the attack. We weren't able to do much, other than defend the station from a secondary attack by mortar or gunfire from snipers. We took cover as best we could and monitored the station perimeter.

At first light, I started piecing together what had happened. Six mortars had been launched from the community centre in the village towards the police station (the community centre is about 180 yards away). Luckily the third mortar in the launch tube stuck and when it exploded it took the rest of the mortars with it; there was only two that landed in the station.

Thirty years in the police and my main recurring memory is that visit to the toilet. Nobody was killed or seriously injured.

As a result of this incident, feeling dazed and 'unusual' I reported to my Doctor. I was put on sick leave and unable to perform duties required. Exactly 3 weeks after this incident another mortar attack was launched on the station. Four bedrooms destroyed, a direct hit. Mine was one.

Image: Mortar attack Carrickmore, before secure (reinforced concrete) Police Stations were introduced.

Note: These reinforced Police Stations were constructed in "special category police areas" subsequent to a mortar attack in Newry in February 1985 when nine police officers sadly lost their lives.

The Last Great Adventure

(Anon)

Samuel Fox

Whenever we performed prisoner escort duties in the SPG we normally escorted a Prison Van taking a prisoner from Crumlin Road Gaol to another area for a Remand Hearing or whatever.

We got to know most of the motor transport drivers who were usually senior Constables running down the clock for retirement.

Sam Fox had been running down the clock for over 20 years. He had joined early and had 40 years' service when I got talking to him one afternoon in Downpatrick. A quiet man with a keen sense of humour we bonded immediately.

Anyway 1982 in Standtown I had been seconded into the Warrants and Summons office working alongside the one full time member, Constable S.

One morning I compiled my days work, business addresses during the day, private addresses in the late afternoon etc. One stood out – a 'Certificate of Service' to be handed to Constable Samuel Fox, signed by the Chief Constable, in the Orangefield area.

I called late that afternoon. We recognised each other immediately. We had a cup of tea and chatted about the old days. I served him with his certificate and parted, he had been the most senior Police Officer ever in the UK serving 44 years with the force.

CHIEF SUPERINTENDENT HAROLD BREEN
SUPERINTENDENT ROBERT BUCHANAN

'Oh death where is they sting?
O grave where is my victory?'
1 Corinthians Ch15 v55

I had met him on several occasions in his capacity as a Superintendent and the Sub Divisional Commander (SDC) in charge of the Omagh Police area and its satellite police stations. He was a quiet man of average height, his stature made slightly rotund by middle age. His facial features portrayed a calm, capable, though I would suggest wary person with cautious, curious slightly narrowing eyes. His hands always clasped on his lap whilst seated.

As part of his duty he arrived once every other month to the base I was in charge of as the Station Sergeant. On those occasions every official Police Station register was inspected, certified as correct and in order and signed by him. Also, every item of police equipment was accounted for including all weapons, all ammunition, radios and batteries confirmed as correct and in order. Sometimes after the formalities were concluded we would retire to my office for some tea and biscuits which I ensured were always available. There he would ask me questions about the general running and feeling about the station members; other times he would ask about my service record and various officers we both might have known. Nothing of a personal nature was ever discussed and he never spoke of himself. So, although these talks were informal to a degree, they had parameters. All I really knew was that he was a devoted family man who was deeply involved with his church.

In 1985 he moved from Omagh to take up the post of 'Staff Officer' in Head Quarters and it was from there he advanced to the position of Border Liaison Officer in the South Armagh area whose duties involved meeting with his counterpart Garda Siochana Officers in the County Louth area south of the border. This was in accordance with a stipulation in the Anglo-Irish Agreement 1986.

On Monday 20 March 1989 around 3.30pm in the afternoon he and Chief Superintendent Harold Breen who had overall command for police in the area was returning from an informal meeting with their counterparts in Dundalk, South of Ireland in Robert Buchanan's car. As they were over the border, they were both unarmed.

On that cold mad March day in mid afternoon they had just returned to the northern side of the border near Jonesborough in 'bandit country' and just outside Forkhill, Co Armagh. In a secluded area, what they would have seen in front of them was a man in Army uniform armed with a rifle and face camouflaged, stopping vehicles on the road along with other 'armed soldiers'. This would have been normal in this area, patrolled by British soldiers at that time. As they slowed behind one of the vehicles already halted in front of them, a white van which was following behind them passed and stopped in a layby nearby. More men dressed in Army uniform spilled out from its side door, but they were also wearing black balaclava or ski masks.

The police officers realised only too late that it was a trap set up by the Provisional IRA to ambush them.

Superintendent Buchanan tried to reverse away from the scene, the windscreen of his red unarmoured Vauxhall Cavalier was peppered several times with gun fire from 2 Armalites and Ruger Mini 14 rifle. He was found shot dead at the seat of his car with his foot still on the accelerator. Eyewitnesses later testified that Chief Superintendent Breen had managed to struggle out of the car whilst waving a white handkerchief to surrender.

After both he and Superintendent Buchanan lay there, they were shot one more time in the head, they were probably already dead.

I did not know Chief Superintendent Breen, but I am aware that he too was a family man in his fifties with 2 children. They were 2 of the most senior officers to be killed in the history of 'The Troubles' in Northern Ireland.

Theories of collusion and breaches of internal security still surround this case. These may be read elsewhere.

The funeral of Superintendent Buchanan was attended by Chief Constable Sir John Hermon and members of the Garda Siochana who were said to have known Mr Buchanan as their friend. The Funeral of Chief Superintendent Breen took place the same day and was similarly attended.

Image: Superintendent Robert Buchannon (left) with myself (right) 1985

CARRICKMORE, CO TYRONE 1985

'The difference between Stupidity and Genius, is that Genius has its limits'
Albert Einstein

Image: Carrickmore 1985 (note: armoured patrol cars)

Route clearances were carried out daily, particularly in rural areas, to determine as far as possible that no improvised explosives devices or landmines had been planted during the night on any of the main arterial roads leading to or from the police station. The intention of the paramilitaries was to set these off by remote control, murdering everyone in a passing police patrol.

One morning, the boys were out on the ground, clearing some of the routes and the main Drumnakilly Road was next to be cleared. Stephen was the Inspector; I was in the office and he was heading into Omagh Station for a meeting. He was only outside Carrickmore about a mile at the most when he came across one of the foot patrols. It was being led by a Sergeant named Bob.

The reality of the route clearances was that you only ever had four or five personnel due to availability and the way they did them was like an inverted V. You had guys out front on the high ground – the top of the V. If there was some terrorist sitting with a transmitter to detonate a bomb the people on the high ground would come upon them – neutralising the threat – while there was no one on the road to be hit by the blast, as they would have been there first. That was the V system. Simple but effective.

Bob, the Sergeant, had been out on a flank for whatever reason and he had been crossing over a barbed wire fence when he saw what looked like a bit of fishing line. What he did next was rather foolish, I suppose. There are no rivers or lakes around there, so a fishing line was completely out of place. He caught hold of this line and gave it a good yank. Luckily, whatever way he did it, the line snapped. Then he walked back along the fence towards the road, to where the fishing wire had been leading, this was just as the Inspector was driving past. The Inspector stopped and they both spotted a concrete water main, the cover of which had been split into two halves. It was a common enough sight in the countryside. As they were having a look at it, they noticed what appeared to be fresh footprints around it.

The next thing, I got a call from the Inspector asking if I could get a crowbar and bring it out to them because they wanted to move this two-part lid to see into the drain to be sure it was safe. It was so ludicrous when you think back – madness but of course I couldn't find a crowbar. I searched all around the station and all I could get was the metal part of a pickaxe but there was no shaft on it. It could act, though, like an improvised crowbar.

When I found them, I jumped out of the car and headed towards them in the field. I could see the other boys were up on the high ground giving cover to us with rifles. The next thing a woman left her nearby house, got into the car and took off. She was in a hurry and very agitated, it thought it was suspicious, but I was still so preoccupied about not having found a crowbar.

We jammed the pointy end of the pick in — if you had had a crowbar you would have slid it across. Across the road they had been building fencing along the road and the workmen had left a pile of those 4x4 paling posts. I suggested if we lifted the metal lid over a bit more, we could put a couple of these posts in, which would help with the light.

Image left: Foot patrol, Carrickmore circa 1984

The Sergeant, the Inspector and I were down on our knees in this field trying to see what's going on. Steve the Inspector, then decided he didn't want to get his hands dirty anymore. The Sergeant and I did all the spadework, literally. We managed to get the cover lifted further up and I was trying to look down into this thing. I thought I saw something that looked a wee bit like insulating tape, blue tape or something. I never thought. The next thing the Inspector is down on his hunkers and he goes, "Holy fuck, run!" That wasn't something we needed to be told twice. Off we went and boy did we run!!

I was off weekends back then. I used to work 5 days on and 2 off, it was a Friday, so I'd be going off for the weekend. As it happened it was Friday 13 January! I couldn't wait to get away. I headed for home as soon as I got back to the station. Later that night I was out down the town having a beer with some mates and this big fellow who worked in Carrickmore Station as well, walked in. He was off on his rest days and he came up to me in the bar and said, "Did you hear the news?" I said, "No, what's happened now?" He said, "You know that suspect device thing you were at this morning? It was a 600lb land mine!" "You're fucking joking", I said, "No, I'm afraid I'm not!" he said. The terrorists had taken fright when they saw the police coming towards them doing the formation. They didn't run a wire, but they had like a clothes peg with a dolly pin in it and the 2 connectors. Their plan was they'd pull it out with the fishing line, which would complete the connection, but they had panicked and scarpered. Luckily for the Sergeant, when he pulled the line it broke so the dolly was still in the clothes peg and it didn't go off.

With hindsight I have no doubt that women who left the house and drove away when she saw us at the drain cover knew exactly what was going on and that there was a bomb there. She was happy enough to have us blown to smithereens, but she didn't have the stomach to see or hear it. It was pure luck we survived.

Image: Site of old Police Station, Carrickmore 2019

ROSSLEA MASSIVE LANDMINE 1984 EXPLOSION

"Death, A Necessary End, Will Come When it May Come"
William Shakespeare – Julius Ceasar

Image: Security Sanger Joint RUC/Army Security Camp 1984

Another incident that happened in Roslea a couple of years later, when I was a Sergeant there in early '84. Some things you just can't explain or maybe some things are best left unexplained.

A few of us were living in the station and about 4am one morning there was an almighty explosion. Everyone woke up wondering what it was. The whole area was immediately placed 'out of bounds', i.e. closed to any security forces pending investigation into what had happened; in case of secondary devices. In the morning light we got an armed helicopter to fly over the area to see what exactly had happened. They could see the road had been blown apart as the result of a massive land mine explosion between Roslea and Fivemiletown. We didn't know if it was, what we would call, an own goal. In other words, blowing themselves up when planting the device or whatever, we didn't know.

There was a policeman in the station who didn't drive and every Monday he used to get the bus down to Fivemiletown and the police car went up to collect him. It transpired that the bomb was designed for the police car that afternoon, going to collect him and bring him into work. When the ATO (Army Technical Officer), and the Bomb Disposal Officer came to examine scene, there was no sign of any bodies. This was strange because if this device had gone off prematurely, when it was being planted, there should have been. It had obviously been set properly with a view to murdering police, but it remained a bit of a mystery as to what exactly had occurred.

About a month or so later I was out with the army on foot patrol across the fields where the explosion had occurred and there was an aul boy who lived there with his brother, a farmer. I got chatting to him and he invited us in for a cup of tea. As is always the case, the locals know everything first. The old boy said to me, "that woman was very lucky there, three or four weeks ago". I didn't want to appear stupid, so I said something vaguely, "Oh aye, she was lucky all right". I didn't want to show my hand and then he said, "If she had been there a couple of seconds earlier, that car of hers would have been blown off the road and her with it". I nodded.

Apparently, the woman had been up visiting relatives in Cooneen, outside the area and was on her way back to Roslea at the time these boys had been setting up the ambush. It was the dead of night and she was driving a Mk4 Ford Cortina which was the type police would use often in that area. Probably all they saw was the shape of the car in the headlights, they knew it was a Mk4 Cortina and they presumed it was maybe the police out on patrol.

Rather than take a chance if they had been seen or not, the bombers thought well, we'll just detonate it and leave, which is exactly what they did.

A very lucky escape for all of us.

Image: View of Roslea Village 2019

Image: View of Roslea Village 1984

Image: Gardening at Roslea 1984

Image: Front Entrance of what was the Police Station today, a Builders Yard

ATTACK ON RECRUITS

"But screw your courage to the sticking place and we'll not fail"
Shakespeare - MacBeth

Enniskillen Mobile Support Unit (MSU) 1980 - 1982

Fermanagh in 1980 held the unenviable statistic of having the greatest number of deaths in any divisional area in Northern Ireland (NI). Many members of the Army and Police (full time and part time members) had been shot and blown up in booby trap devices along with several civilians. Off duty part time security force members were particularly vulnerable whilst working at their regular civilian jobs as van drivers, delivery men, school bus drivers, teachers, farmers and civil servants due to the necessity of habitual routines.

Our patrol area was County Fermanagh and parts of County Tyrone, both situated to the south west of the province of Northern Ireland. Fermanagh is divided in half by Lower and Upper Lough Erne which are framed by the rest of the county. These loughs are fed by the Erne River which eventually flows into the Atlantic Ocean. It is also connected to the River Shannon via a waterway which in turn flows via Athlone and then to Limerick, both in the Republic.

The 'L' Division MSU had hastily been formed in 1980 and consisted of a core of men who were either from nearby, single officers and other souls who had transgressed through work in some way. The Senior Officers and Sergeants formed the nucleus of MSU throughout Northern Ireland, whose duties did not appeal to everyone, nor indeed to the members who had been seconded into it against their will.

Some of these conscripted men included 'loners'; gamblers; overly active social acolytes; divorced officers and young single men who had been uprooted from the familiarity of home and police areas and banished to these MSU's in the outbacks. I was different because of boredom and an unfortunate incident to stay one step ahead of the posse, I knew I had only two realistic options – apply for this, or if it in time proved fruitless, then the Foreign Legion!

Some of the latter 'press-ganged' new arrivals truly seemed shell shocked, preferring to spend long spells on their own, with others seen muttering to themselves surrounded by tins of 'dead soldiers', colourfully entitled Mad Dog 20/20, Tennents Extra, Blitzkrieg Imported ale or popular old staples of Buckfast and Mundies fine wine. Such tortured soles also enquiring "Where the fuck can you get Mundies on a Tuesday!" or ruefully telling anyone about them of 'How things used to be….'

Whatever the reason for these mens' transfers it did, in no way, seem to deter nor quell their thirsts or desires to master the art of drinking!

Accommodation consisted of 12 men living in two former dormitories of the Training Centre in Enniskillen, which was situated by the lake and opposite to a mostly nationalist Cornagrade housing estate on the other side of the lake. I had known police who were from this housing estate and never being able to visit their relatives for fear of being attacked! My humble abode was a caravan in a car park behind the canteen, my only luxury being a duck down sleeping bag.

The other 12 or so had already been established in the county and thus had acquired a solid working knowledge of it. This 'local knowledge' was invaluable.

We were a motley, but rugged hard-core unit of men (mostly!) more akin to the Army in demeanour and dress, often returning to base after long hours outdoors caked in mud, sweat, unshaven and unruly; the antithesis of those in training.

I once met a recruit, in the shared isolation of our combined protected barracks, who I went to school with. He was immaculate in his best dress uniform and shiny boots, regulation short back and sides haircut and crowned with a new RUC forage hat. I was the opposite, socks pulled up over long Military Army regulation boots, my hair much too long and returning to secure my personal SLR rifle in the armoury. I had no cap and sported an Army issue green neck scarf around my neck, hiding my mint green shirt. As protection against the elements, I was still wearing a fern green rubberised over suit, waterproof trousers and jacket. I looked more like an artificial inseminator than a Police Officer.

We spoke for a while; I had just arrived back from an area search and his time was restricted. As we parted he smiled and whispered, "You know Willie, we are not really allowed to associate with you boys, the Instructor said just 'ignore them' as you were all a bunch of miscreants who were too recalcitrant for normal duties and best kept well away from: examples of what dames, drink, high life and debt could do …" I just burst out laughing.

My mate, Mad Dog McCrea and I wrote a little song of several verses which we sang to the tune of Eddie Cochrane's Summertime Blues which goes as follows: -

"Here's the story of the DMSU, I know it well, but I'll sing it to you.
Well I used to be in Belfast but now I'm down here,
I'm living with McKenzie and it's driving me queer!
I don't know what I'm a going to do, for there ain't no cure

for the Alcatraz Blues"

Priceless.

I knew that our area was dangerous for all security forces. Indeed, whilst I was earlier stationed in Dundonald, I had to accompany the Sergeant from Rosslea to the family of Constable Joe Rose, an RUC officer who had been in the last Hotspur* to leave the station along with Constable Winston Howe. This vehicle had been blown off the main Lisnaskea/Roslea Road by a **'culvert' bomb. Both officers were killed. The Sergeant had the unenviable task of informing the Rose family, who lived in our area, of the tragic news of Joe's death.

Enniskillen town itself, although it had its share of shootings and some bombing of commercial properties, was generally quiet. It was and still is the capital of Fermanagh if you like and its geography being on a small island and serviced by bridges made it ideal seated in the centre of the county. It also was home to Enniskillen Castle dating back to the 16th century. It now houses the Fermanagh County Museum and Enniskillen Fusiliers Museum.

Sadly, later in 1987 on Remembrance Sunday it's Cenotaph was the scene of an atrocity which was condemned by all except the perpetrators and their few supporters.

The first emergency call I attended was to the attempted murder of track suited recruits making their way on foot to Enniskillen local leisure centre's swimming pool.

armoured landrover
** *a culvert bomb is a river drain which passes under a road, large enough to crawl through or pack explosives into*

On the morning of the incident we had not yet commenced duty. I was at home in the comfort of my caravan when I heard the explosion and saw the cloud of smoke rise about a quarter to half a mile away.

We were all immediately called to duty, the only exceptions were members away on private business. We quickly donned some official uniform clothing and sped to the scene.

It was obvious the device had been placed near a gap where the students would pass by. Fortunately, although there were not any fatalities, some were badly injured. The culprits, as usual, had fled however within 30 minutes the Sergeant in charge of a nearby village police station requested for immediate backup.

On a hunch, he had been on duty with a young Constable (later Inspector who I came to know well in Training Branch).

He suspected the terrorist might go through his area so he and the Constable set up a two man road stop on a minor road in the vicinity of Tempo, where he served as local Sergeant for many years.

Soon they heard a motorcycle approaching. It was June time and the weather was beautiful. As the motorcycle rounded a bend in the road towards them, there was no exit. He observed its pillion passenger throw an article over the hedge row. The Sergeant drew his ruger revolver and the Constable with him raised his M1 Carbine rifle and demanded the bike to stop. He questioned and detained them there until further police were summoned.

On the initial search the object thrown was quickly found and identified as the remote-control activation device that triggered the bomb.

The two suspects were arrested, isolated and taken to Enniskillen Police Station for questioning. I was summoned as gaoler to ensure the older of the two was handcuffed and detained in an office. I remember just he and I facing each other. He never once lifted his gaze from the floor in front of him.

This, at 21 years of age, was to be the first time I had set my eyes on an active terrorist caught red handed. It was not to be long before I came face to face with Provisional Irish Republican Army (PIRA) Active Service Unit (ASU).

Image: MSU Enniskillen circa 1981 (note unmarked police car)

FATAL SHOOTING - DERRYGONNELLY, 1980

"Out, out brief candle"
William Shakespeare - Macbeth (Act 5 Scene 5)

It was a cold clear evening in November 1980 at 7pm when two cars containing six armed officers pulled over to set up a vehicle checkpoint on the main Enniskillen to Derrygonnelly Road and two miles from the village which nestles in the heart of County Fermanagh.

Derrygonnelly is a small village containing a few shops, a Police Station and a local pub. It was a place which had been relatively untouched, thus far, by terrorism.

The Police Station in the village was manned periodically each day for two hours to enable members of the public to produce driving documents, firearms certificates and any other queries of a general police nature.

It should be noted that these minor police posts although not heavily fortified were surrounded on their perimeters by the usual metal poles and security wire. The entrance gate to which was electronically operated. It was also protected from all sides by CCTV to enable the officer to identify unannounced callers from outside and from the safety of the inner enquiry office.

At 7pm all our crew were out of the vehicles and positioned as trained that is to say 2 rifle men at either side of the body of men stopping vehicles approximately 50 yards apart.

It so happened that a member of the public, at exactly that time, was exiting Derrygonnelly Police Station having been on a private matter. He exited across the road and walked towards the direction of a row of Council houses, 2 of which were occupied by Police officers working in the area.

As he strolled, he would have been illuminated by the orange security lights on the perimeter of the police compound. He made his way along the footpath towards his parked vehicle when 2 gunmen hiding in a hedge, a matter of feet from him, opened fire with automatic rifles striking him a number of times. He was riddled at point blank range and fatally wounded. As he lay half on the footpath and the road one of the terrorists then came out from his hiding place and again shot him in the back of the head, this time with a handgun.

It was a case of mistaken identity, the intended target being the Policeman inside the station who should have been leaving at that time. Mr Donaldson was a 59-year-old protestant with 8 children who was from the Erne Terrace in Derrygonnelly and had been in the station collecting for a hospital charity. In a cruel twist of fate his friend John James Dundas, a 65-year-old protestant with 6 of a family suffered a fatal heart attack as he was driving past the Derrygonnelly Police station where his friend, Mr. Donaldson, had just been murdered and crashed his car.

We clearly heard the staccato high velocity shots which sounded very similar to a Kangol pneumatic drill hammer used for digging up roads. The single shot was immediately identified by us as a low velocity shot. We knew exactly what was occurring a short distance from us.

Unspoken all 6 of us climbed into the unmarked Police cars and sped off in the direction. As I drove the powerful Toyota Crown Saloon Sergeant 'N' beside me reported the incident to HQ via radio emergency.

As we rushed towards the Derrygonnelly Main Street, not 2 minutes away, we were acutely aware that we could also become targets.

"Delta from LD 155, 155 & 156 en route, ETA one minute" "Roger 155, proceed to area of LG with extreme caution, report of a shooting incident there" confirmed the radio controller in a soft slow commanding voice, his delivery conveying the severity of the incident.

No two tones. No sirens. Headlights off. The well-practiced fashion. The road was mostly straight and reflected some light from the moon and heavens above.

On approach I slowed from 100mph to 10mph without locking the brakes or screeching the tyres on this starlit evening, as we slowly approached the village.

I knew the second Police car was directly behind me; I could see their faces in the illumination from my brake lights.

The village was in darkness, but the scene was illuminated by the warm orange glow of the security lighting from the Police station as it fell onto the road and footpath outside its boundary.

"Stop her here Cleek", commanded my Sergeant upon us seeing what appeared to be a large sack of potatoes spilling from the footpath onto the road. I jumped out and grabbed my SLR self-loading 7.62mm rifle which was resting between the seat and the door, it's magazine downwards. In one swift well-rehearsed motion, I cocked and pointed it forwards with both hands, safety off, ready to fire.

I crouched and ran towards a strategic corner to my right whilst looking for secondary devices on the ground or waste bins nearby.

Sergeant 'N' remained in radio contact whilst the other 4 officers in a well-rehearsed manner had grabbed their rifles and darted into darkness in order to provide firing cover for 360 degrees circle if needed.

I crouched at the gable wall of a house. My heart was pounding in stereo and my mouth was dry as I tried to control my breathing as trained. My senses tingling. I smelt the lingering odour of cordite and burnt gunpowder in the stillness of the cold, crisp, still night air. The smell was as familiar as blue cheese from constant weapon and anti-ambush training on the firearm ranges and it fuelled the adrenalin which had kicked in.

Through my personal radio I could hear Sergeant 'N' requesting immediate backup from behind the relative safety of the Toyota's engine block. It's amazing how everything clicks as a result of repeated live training.

Then a strange calmness or tranquillity suggesting everything was going to be fine for me. I had originally felt this sensation whilst working in Belfast SPG after a bomb had exploded.

It's as if the mind is separate and detached as everything goes into slow motion almost watching someone else in my place.

(Anyone who has survived a serious car or motorcycle accident and survived, will have felt this for sure.)

A short while later, when we had established there were no secondary devices, Constable McC slowly approached the scene and confirmed it was a human body, beyond first aid recovery. Nothing was touched pending the arrival of specialist services.

The whole scene was made more confusing by a crashed vehicle which had happened at the same time.

When further support arrived, I was detailed as Scene Log Officer to ensure the whole area was not contaminated by other persons. Only those documented and sanctioned by myself were allowed to enter the primary area.

I remained at my post and these duties until 3:30am after Scenes of Crime Officers, Photographers, Mapping and Detectives had left.

Much discussion back at base but everyone retired to their quarters around first light.

Another macabre image etched for eternity. Families, relatives and friends left behind to grieve.

My Senior Friend

Andrew William Beacom, Drew Beacom and I became firm friends when I first arrived in County Fermanagh in May of 1980. I was assigned to his crew, which was the second vehicle and C Section Division on a Mobile Patrol Unit in Enniskillen. There were six constables and a sergeant, Sergeant Nelson (RIP), who was in charge. Although in our team Sergeant Nelson, or 'Shorter Length Parting' as we call him, really left the running of things to us, which suited everyone perfectly. So; our consultant, as it were, made more important decisions such as where we were all to regroup for beers after the shift. Oddly enough, he was the only one married. Two car crews thus consisted of 'Shorter Length Parting' (Sergeant Nelson), 'Terrible Tim', Herbie 'Tell us an aul yarn', 'Baaa' McKay, 'Smokey', 'Mad Dog' and me 'Cleeky'. We were joined later on by another member named Jay who was christened 'Space Invader Head'. Anyway, I wonder what happened to him?

Drew 'Smokey' Beacom was the most senior of the constables by far. At that time he was not married and, I would have thought, about 33 or 34 years of age. He used to regale us of tales in the early 70s when he was stationed in Mountpottinger, East of Belfast. He came from County Tyrone, on the County Fermanagh borders and had served his earlier years in Belfast as, was then customary, for single officers. He was a huge lump of a country man, he knew the areas we were working, probably and arguably better than anyone else in our unit or indeed in Enniskillen. Just as sergeant Don P in Dundonald Station had educated me in the ways of the 'townies', Big Drew reciprocated and instructed me in the way of the, 'culchies'.

Really I had a foot in each camp because, being from Newtownards, originally, I was just on the periphery of Belfast and really for someone local to Fermanagh, anybody North or North East of the Steinmore roundabout in Dungannon would have been classified as a 'townie'. However, I was mostly his driver and the second of two unmarked cars patrolling our area. Although quiet and easy going, talking slow and deliberately only when necessary, he could be quite impatient and abrupt when asked his thoughts on, what he thought to be inane or unnecessary questions. Accordingly, my humour being what it was, I asked these regularly for fun to provoke a reaction. Whilst on cross country border foot patrols he and I always paired it off on these arduous all terrain, day and night patrols. Normally we were dropped off either in a plain clothed or covert vehicle, like a van, or by Army or RAF helicopters in remote and high risk areas or sensitive areas not accessible by road due to the fact that some of the roads went through the South and then back into the North. I'm sure I've learned as much about the flora and fauna and geographical aspects of this beautiful County Fermanagh as I have the more relevant and necessary local knowledge which everyone required. Of course, we were aware that the threat of gun, bomb, or rocket attack was there continually and took every precaution. We were trained regularly in anti-ambush techniques and drills and we tried to familiarise ourselves with these tactics as best we could, which was invaluable on many occasions.

On a two-car mobile patrol, it was accepted both statistically and generally that if there was a landmine attack it was odds on the second vehicle would be the target. This was not always the case in the event of a gun attack, as was my colleague Tim could well attest to, whilst being involved in a gun attack some two or three years later when it was the first vehicle that was under attack, he was very lucky to survive.

On reflection, in my total of seven years on two separate attachments to the southwest and west of the province were amongst the finest and most enjoyable days of my service in the Royal Ulster Constabulary. After leaving 'L Division', as it was called then, for the second time in 1986, I never saw my friend Drew Beacom again. Tragically on 12th December 1993 whilst he was on a mobile patrol in the Fivemiletown area of County Tyrone, on the Fermanagh border where he was from, with reserve constable Ernie Smith, "my senior friend", as I always referred to him, was shot dead while approaching a road junction. He was only 46. Drew's funeral was a large affair. It was, of course, emotional to meet my old colleagues from County Fermanagh and from 'L Division' in general, so much so, that I left quietly after the ceremony. Gone but not forgotten.

Image: Constable Andrew/Drew W Beacon, Belcoo 1981 with unmarked policec ar (Renault 18 Turbo)

Myths & Legends

"Fool me once, shame on ...
Shame on you.
Fool me, you can't get fooled again" (sic).
George W. Bush

Sergeant P 6303

"Beauty like a shadow flies and our youth before us dies"
Robert Anderson

I never found out his Christian name. The Unit Inspector and other Sergeants referred to him as Sergeant P in his presence or sometimes 'Nat' when out of ear shot, although his proper Christian name was neither Nathan nor Nathanial. He had acquired his nickname very early on in his time in the RUC; most probably in the post war years when he first arrived at a rural/country barracks, far away from his native Belfast. (In those years a police officer was not permitted to serve in his home county or that of his wife's should he become married).

There was always an endearing banter between members of the greater Belfast area ('townies' or 'Sammy's') and the other members who were not – (Farmers/Culchies).

At Sergeant 'P's' new posting the other constables and officers who were already working there were continually ragging him. They would frequently ask this young constable if his Christian name was 'Richard', 'Bob; 'William', or whatever wrong name sprung to mind. Now, being a 'townie', his accent/dialect was different from rural areas so when repeatedly asked he got fed up and replied, 'it's not', his accent greatly amused them, his annunciation sounded to them "it's Nat"! So, when anyone else asked the name of the new constable, those who already knew him continued to tell others "Oh that's Nat".

'Hoist with his own petard'. He always had a swift riposte for any problem. I remember Constable Coll-er-ooo overslept one morning. He knew he would be in for a tongue lashing from him, so when he parked his old wreck of a car in the yard, I opened the bonnet (hood), took out the oil dip-stick and smeared some dirty oil over his hands. He entered the bunker, claimed his car had broken down and showed Nat his dirty hands as proof. Nat dismissed his excuse telling him that he should have risen early enough to walk to work and still arrive on time!

I knew that despite him outwardly pretending to acknowledge that everyone else was just a fool, he quite liked me even though he once informed me that the recruiting officer who signed me up should be 'sacked for neglect of duty'!!

I remembered the last time I saw him. It was around 8 or 9 years later when he had retired, and I was back on patrol as a Sergeant in the Belfast area. He appeared from nowhere as an apparition one day on the pavement before me in Belfast city centre. A broad smile on his face and hand outstretched he exclaimed, "Hello son! You've done ok for yourself, good for you, knew you would! Never forget, there's gougers (street corner boys) running around these parts receiving a pension out of that job", (a direct reference to himself).

MUSGRAVE STREET - BELFAST CITY CENTRE

"We are the sum total of our memories. Memories are the most previous things we have"
Anon

Image: Saturday night patrol from Musgrave Street, front entrance circa early 1900s

I think they're all gone now. Perhaps some of the later ones built in the sixties and onwards survived, but certainly all the "border outposts" I served in during the late seventies and eighties have vanished in all but memory. It's a bitter-sweet melancholy of sadness that I feel.

Enniskillen remains and is, as such as a sentinel to the gates of the past. Mount Pottinger and Musgrave street "barracks" on either side of the River Lagan in Belfast, recently were confined to history and its mediums. Gone too are all the 'aul hands' who populated the hidden corners of these bastions. 'Old men' then probably in their late forties, or even fifties, who were rarely seen from Monday to Friday or during the hours between 9am and 5pm when these phantoms were, someone said, regularly there and never at weekends or public holidays when they, as usual, rested.

Occasionally we caught a glimpse of one of these spectres, scampering from one hidey hole to the next, assuming an air of self-importance uniformly dressed as always in slacks, loafers, shirts and ties and always with that mandatory sheet of paper held, conspicuously, to the fore in one hand. The other rubbing their chin or running it their hand through their hair, if there was any and armed with one of those official issue black police pens in the other. Perhaps a spare back up pencil angled behind their ear, only used in extreme emergencies. I often wondered, what exactly did they do? The rumours suggested that they were police constables, but no one knew for sure. If so, what was their job? No one really knew.

Image: Motor Transport Division, Musgrave Street RIC

The motor transport department in Musgrave Street Police Station was found hiding under a canopy of systematically angled glass windows, which were supported by a quadrangle of smooth clay, red baked bricks of the kind never seen nowadays but prevalent in the Victorian days of the late nineteenth and early twentieth centuries. Along with being the main police station for Belfast City Centre it was also the 'mothership' for a legion of these senior constables put out to graze in the latter parts of their careers, mostly drivers for Motor Transport Department. Ironically it had originally been used for other types of grazing, the horses were stabled there to pull uniformed carts of policemen or supplies around Belfast to and from the docks, or other areas as required and also on those special occasions when a dignitary or royalty descended to grace us. I used to take my car into its bowels for a wash. Under the glass canopy were now stabled and paraded lines of light grey Ford transit police personnel vans, their anonymity only portrayed by different registration numbers on the front and back. Their 'in transit' cargo of police officers being ferried across the province to parades and demonstrations were protected from outside elements by sheets of plastic perspex over the windows, not bullet or bomb proof, but rock, catapult and bottle resistant. There were also found, the dark blue transit vans whose cargo normally were ferried between the jail and courthouse and back for hearings of remand or sentencing. I got to know many of these old characters, their sanctumsantori was a portacabin inside of which they languished. Most only needed six hours of sleep daily and another eight hours at night. Those not recumbent stood around guarding an old superser gas heater burning on three bars in the middle. Their dreary depressing monotone monologues range between 'how things used to be' or 'how the aul job's fucked' or 'tales of rabble rousing around the old dance halls in the fifties (high on lemonade and ice cream purveyed therein, I should imagine)'. Their discourse solemnly punctuated sometimes by news that 'Head Constable such and such died last week' then qualified by an assassination of the departed's charter and also that he had a serving son, a Sergeant, in Benburb or some other instantly forgettable hamlet and whose parentage was equally questionable.

I have learned quickly that a 'cub' like me – a mere 30 years of age – had no right, business nor qualifications to offer any input. It provoked a soft whisper of the wind, which broke my induced deadly silence. Then much ear poking, close scrutiny of the finger for evidence, followed by frowning and coded sideways glances.

Oh, Bob was the most convivial, he was their Sergeant and was due to retire 20 years ago. He told me a memorable incident whilst he was a young constable on 'beat patrol' duties around the docks area of Belfast. One evening he was told to go to where there was a report of men on some waste ground, according to a night watchman – and they were making a nuisance.

On his arrival he saw perhaps eight or ten homeless men passing bottles of cheap alcohol between themselves, standing around a metal drum brazier, which was spitting sparks high into the cosmic abyss above. He enquired what they might be doing? In typical 'black' Belfast humour, one flickering orange faceless silhouette reposted,
"We're having a wine and cheese party, but we've run out of cheese".

They're not around anymore, those old folk from generations ago. The world has moved on, spinning quicker now having ejected these characters into space, or has it?

When I was a young recruit/student, I remember vividly a Staff Instructor trying to imbue us with the notion that 'The Job' as we always referred to it, was 'finished', doomed, not like what it used to be, gone too modern perhaps? He even went as far as suggesting this genesis began around about 1968 with the abolishment of The Larceny Act and its successor, The Theft Act!

Image: *Fergal* *O'Hanlon* *and* *Sean* *South* *Monument,* *Brookborough*

Image: Fergal O'Hanlon and Sean South Monument, Brookborough

He regaled us about his part in the defence of an IRA attack on Brookeborough RUC Station on January 1st, 1957 and its long-term ramifications. I remember calculating his age to be about 50 and thus, should he not be retired? Then I gradually learned that with increase in years' service on 'The Job' earned gratuitous lamenting. At that time, everything was new to us and we couldn't quite fathom his reasoning. The then current period of unrest in Northern Ireland had not been going for 10 years – maybe he was frightened of the future?

Interestingly, as I approached 22 years of police service, my thoughts were beginning to echo his at that time. My reflections on how things had changed almost imperceptibly though relentlessly during my time in 'The Job' and now as an 'impartial observer' detached from its vagaries almost as long out of it, as in it.

Perhaps 'The job' is a working continuum, whose shelf-life spans somewhere between 20 and 25 years from 'seeking the bubble reputation' as far as its demise via 'slippered pantaloons' to retirement? I don't know, I still have very fond memories.

Image: Musgrave Street, Officers on Patrol circa 1950

Image: Early RUC Officers Dundrum, Co Down 1922

'KOWOLSKI'

'The babe in the woods'

"I speak 4 languages fluently and a little English". That's what he told me when I asked. He had been born in Poland and had met his wife whilst at University in France. They subsequently fell in love and she brought him back to her native Northern Ireland as a husband.

He had had several manual labouring jobs before joining the RUC, which was 1973 I believe. In those early years he was in the process of learning English. He told me that one of his first jobs was working on a building site in the Belfast area. This was in the very early stages of 'the troubles' and as you can imagine his presence there was a source of great curiosity to local tradesman and labourers with whom he worked. Political correctness was not, in those days, as it should have been. The innate Belfast/NI humour prevailed on many occasions. All of the local slang, jargon and epithets would have been unfamiliar to him, but he managed the best he could, his English language improving daily. However, not all the new language would have augured well with his wife, who indeed attended Mass with her husband 'religiously'.

Once in a vain effort to impress his wife with his skills and fluency in English, at teatime he returned with some new vocabulary that day. When he sat down to eat his tea he asked of his wife "Where is my fuckin tea? Are you fuckin me about or what?" this did not go down well and he subsequently found himself working in the capacity of a trainee Lay Preacher which his wife opined was much more fitting. However, some of the local vernacular still puzzled him.

I remember vividly on one occasion whilst we were driving round the old Smithfield Market of Belfast, he spied a former Lay Preacher from his former employment. "Stop. Stop the Rover" he ordered in his strong Balkan accent. I pulled over to the kerb and stopped the vehicle. He flung open his passenger side door, donned his cap and as he alighted from the vehicle with his hand outstretched, he greeted this individual with "How ya doin ye 'aul bollocks ye!" Eruptions from within, officers in the rear diving in hiding on the floor!

He used to talk to me about his home life fondly and often, it seemed as if I was his confidante as I drove him along on patrol. He once asked me if I was married? I was not and never had been but seized the opportunity gleefully. "Not anymore". He looked at me aghast and asked my age. I truthfully answered, "21". Then he asked, "How long were you married", I entered into character and replied, "Just long enough to consummate the divorce". "What!, What??" he exploded. "What on earth happened", I continued in my new persona and ventured to tell him I had discovered, all too late, that my wife had been a lady of low moral standings, unbeknown to me at that time. "Where is the girl now?", "Girl? Girl??, she is 44", I announced and galvanized it with "She's back working round the Albert Clock", I replied straight faced as we drove along. I tried to focus on the road ahead in my valiant bid not to laugh.

(The Albert Clock was one of the few areas around the Docks area of Belfast where ladies of a particular calling purveyed the second oldest profession in the world. (It was in Musgrave Street Police Station area where my Sergeant had previously worked as a constable).

"But, but this is ridiculous, you must try and find her, you're bound by your holy vows as man and wife, in sickness and in health" "Hooker" I murmured. He ordered me to drive back to base. As I glanced in the rear-view mirror of the armoured Landrover, I saw 6 legs kicking frantically in the dark gloom with back doors being closed. As it was near quitting time when we arrived at base it is the driver's duty to complete the vehicle's logbook including miles covered and petrol used etc. I was completing this task when one of my colleagues said, "The Inspector wants to see you, "Yeah dead on", I sneered. This was a frequent ploy used for mischief. "No joking, you better get in there Willie, it looks serious".

He seemed genuine, so I put down the logbook and wandered through to our Inspector's office. The sight which greeted me was not encouraging. There sat the Inspector behind his desk facing me to the right of which stood a very efficacious looking Sergeant R, in full uniform, hat on his head and standing rigidly to attention staring at the wall in front of him.

I gulped, blinked and swallowed hard. Twice. "Well Constable", the inspector began. "What's all this I hear about abandoning your wife and putting her out to walk the streets?". I couldn't speak. I daren't. I stared at the wall in front of me and tried not to breathe. I shrugged my shoulders a little and tried to acknowledge his question but all I could muster was a short snort like a pig and another shrug of my shoulders. This was a carbon copy of the Roman Centurion sketch from a Monty Python film, 'The Life of Brian'. The stare from behind the desk seemed to continue for months. Presently though, the Inspector who had also managed to keep it together slid his hooded eyes from me to the Sergeant and back again, "Willie" he declared "You are a fekin' eejit and more's the fool to you Rudy for listening to him. Dismissed".

Sergeant R wouldn't speak to me for days and it was only when I purloined him a couple of steaks from my father's fridge-freezer this his coolness to me thawed as they defrosted.

In memory of Inspector Kasimirez Rudewizi (Rudi)
died peacefully in hospital on 17th August 2020
RIP   Rest Peacefully Brother – Your Duty is Done!

Benny, My Name

'Great souls by instinct to each other turn, demand alliance and in friendship burn'
Joseph Addison

I knew him from before I joined the RUC. I met him through my sister and brother-in-law who in turn had met him in Downpatrick where his relatives were from. Someone told me that his birthday was April 1st, but I found out over the years that he was nobody's fool – not just because of the intensive look in his eyes but he always listened much more than he spoke.

Curious in his ways, although not directly involved in the ways of the church he was a resolute pioneer and abstained from alcohol (The devil's vomit') however, I did on more than one occasion see him discreetly licking his lips after being teased into a sample of best ale!

I bumped into him infrequently after I joined the Police in 1978, usually once at family Christmas each year and then periodically when I was out walking along the shoreline at home. It was always a pleasure to meet him again and I knew he was glad to see me, we always stopped for a while to catch up. Then, as fate would have it, we ended up working the Rosslea RUC Station area in 1983 and 1984.

He had entered the police service a while after me when he was more mature. He was a popular member amongst the station party never missing a patrol. Due to my commitments he was in the Barracks at different times than me although normally only when I was off on rest days.

He particularly liked the foot patrols when we were picked up and collected by the Army helicopter. On these flights he just wouldn't be quiet! Although the only member who I ever knew to be allowed to sit up in the front with the pilot and co-pilot during the flight, invariably he was the first off upon landing, such was his enthusiasm.

Back in the station he mucked in with all the duties, even the more laborious ones of station security, both static in the security sangers as well as the boundary patrols maintained on foot.

Although he liked to see himself as generally a 'good all-rounder', he was never a cook. He wasn't a 'picky eater' as he ate most things everyone else ate but refused the more exotic fruits such as avocados (we sometimes got them from the Army cooks) and turned his nose up at even the sweet little nectarine oranges, which everyone agreed were delicious.

Then came my offer to transfer to Carrickmore. We had become very close by this point so when I got the go-ahead for him too, he jumped at the offer to work with me and the added bonus of most weekends off.

We had a great 2 year's duty there despite the numerous incidents during 1984, 85 and 86. He seemed to have more of an aversion to the stray cats in the complex, rather than the continual threat of terrorist attacks.

We left in March 1986 when he returned to ordinary patrol duties and I went to Newtownstewart to resume MSU patrols.

Benny died in 1991 aged 14, I loved that wee Springer Spaniel!!

Years after Benny departed and went to that great boneyard in the sky, I bumped into one of our former colleagues from Carrickmore Police Station days. He spoke fondly of the wee lively liver and white Springer Spaniel. I then told him of a very touching tribute held in his honour by all his canine friends after he passed and the little poem they had written about him. It had been passed to me for posterity, I said it was called 'Benny, His Last Post'.

I then recited it;

"All the doggies had a wake, they can from near and far,
some came by motor-bicycle and some by motor-car.
Each doggie entered the banquet hall and each doggie signed the book.
Each doggie hung his asshole, upon his appointed hook.
But one doggie wasn't invited, and it greatly raised his ire,
so he ran into that banquet hall and he loudly shouted, "fire!!!".
This caused great consternation, all the doggies run amuck
and each doggie grabbed an asshole from another doggie's hook.
and that is why you will always see, no matter where you roam,
each doggie sniffs each other's bum, for to see if it's his own!"

Hobos, Tramps & Bums

"Foolery, Sir, doth walk about the orb like the sun. It shines everywhere"
William Shakespeare – Twelfth Night (Act 3 : Scene 1)

Just what exactly is the difference? I don't suppose we have these anymore – or maybe in this age of political correctness they are still around although under different euphemistic guises. As I was drifting through the USA some years ago in an old Ford I had just bought in a junkyard outside NYC, Bob Dylan, who was hosting a radio show from somewhere local defined the three thus:

- 'Hobo' – a person who moved around from town to town seeking work.
- 'Tramp' – although this person roams from town to town, they are not interested in work.
- 'Bum' – does neither.

Which is the introduction for our story.

There were 3 older men, that everyone knew, in my hometown when I was growing up in the 60's and 70's. Although strictly speaking they wouldn't have fallen into one of these 3 groups, these elderly men were just different, 'loners' I suppose.

They were always out and about in the town although for some strange reason you would never see them together and indeed it was rare to even see 2 of them in the one day. Perhaps, like the Police, they had 3 shifts? i.e., earlies, lates and nights – each covering an eight-hour stint patrolling our streets? They were colourfully nicknamed, Charlie Hawk (pictured right, King Street, Belfast c1970), Willie Woodbine and Eddie – 'The Bike'. The first 2 were not even slightly sociable, indeed, when seen and greeted by me and my peers their response would often direct us to go away and attempt coitus with 2 parts of our own anatomy or 'shit' in its nominative or transitive form. However, Eddie 'the Bike' was totally approachable. He was always friendly and jovial, readily handing out an endless supply of Foxes Glacier Mints, which genuinely kind people could do with total impunity in those days.

Although he always wore cycle clips, a French 'onion-seller's' beret and those little round black spectacles favoured by Groucho Marx, whilst pushing a Victorian-era bicycle around the town on his travels, he never actually rode it. Perhaps he brought it with him in order to carry the little black notebook and stationery hidden in the depths of its cavernous saddle bag. He filled this notebook diligently upon licking the pencil point at each supposed transgression of cars he thought had run a red traffic light in his patrol area. Some older lads suggested he had been shell-shocked during the First World War in Northern France but, when asked as to his purpose Eddie maintained, "I'm just doing my job".

Which brings us conveniently to Bob Baxter from Omagh in the County of Tyrone. I was regaled about this gent by a man called Raymond in a small bar in the village of Beragh also in County Tyrone.

Dressed in the regulation fashion of a farmhand in a rural farming area, that of blue boiler suit, black rubber wellington style boots (turned down at the top) and a brightly coloured woollen hat, modelled perhaps on a tea cosy. Although now an inventor, he once worked formally in the then Tyrone and Fermanagh Mental Institution 30 years previously. It was here that Bob Baxter resided. He told me that Bob had no next of kin when seen living and wandering the streets of Omagh prior to his admission. He had been dwelling in a mud hut which he had built out on the main road towards Cookstown and living on the kindness of others. Raymond also told me Bob was not initially keen in joining the other inhabitants at the institution and only acceded when offered a bed, food and the promise of work as a gardener inside its walls. When I asked Raymond what was his position he claimed to be 'A type of doctor but in a slightly shorter white coat' (in real terms I would suggest his equipment (if indeed ANY!) comprised of something to render the patient harmless to himself or others, handcuffs and possibly a strait jacket).

Bob had settled in well, although he preferred to disassociate himself from the other certified 'residents' having classed them to Raymond under the collective phrase, "A bunch of fuckin' eejits". Person(s) of questionable abilities.

Spring turned to summer and summer languished into the 'Season of mists and mellow fruitfulness'.

With the impending visit of Sir Basil Brooke (the then prime Minister of NI), everyone excitedly geared up to ensure the whole complex was spic and span. Bob happily exchanged his old clothing similar to that of Raymond as he stood at the bar) – for a brand-new ensemble. Then just prior to the arrival of Sir Brooke and his entourage everyone was paraded in the main assembly hall and briefed. When Bob was singularly instructed just to 'carry on as normal' his reply was,
"I'll not be bothering with him as long as he doesn't bother with me".

The formal day duly arrived and the Governers, doctors and staff completed the body of the slinking serpent, who's head consisted of Mr Brooke and company.

A sense of normal normality prevailed as the entourage weaved its way through the various indoor facilities of the red brick building and thence out and into the grounds on that crisp Autumn morning.

Then, disaster. Sir Basil spied the bold Bob Baxter busily sweeping up the falling leaves from the mighty Oak poised on the horizon at the top of the path and putting them into a neat pile. "Who might that be?" queried the Minister to the head of the Institute and within earshot of my narrator Raymond. "Oh, that's Bob Baxter" proudly announced the head honcho "And is he employed here?", further enquired the right Honorable Prime Minister, perhaps in an outrageous bid to claim some glory the honcho said, "Oh no, he's actually one of our patients. We are very proud of his progress here". The Prime Minister paused and then said, "Oh I must meet him". I imagine this was to add credence to his wishes to appear humane and a real 'person of the people' to all gathered and particularly the Press. The procession then made its way along the small meandering path to Bob's lofty position. "Well, my good man, how are you this fine day?", cheerily enquired the leader to Bob who continued to rake the leaves. "Too busy to be talking to the likes of you", he retorted to the horror of those assembled who gasped and tutted amongst themselves.

Undeterred and unruffled and composed Prime Minister countered with, "But, but do you know who I am?".
"No and I care less", remarked a defiant Bob. Sir Basil apparently stood his ground in a mano-a-mano scenario. "I sir, am Sir Basil Brooke, the Prime Minister for Northern Ireland", sprouted Sir Basil in his plummy accent. Once again, the salvo did nothing to deter the defiant Bob. "Well, when you've been in here for a while, you'll soon forget about that". He casually replied.

Image: Homeless person circa 1934

Jerry & Julie

I don't know what became of Willie Woodbine, Charlie Hawke or Eddie, those latter-day Dicken-Sonian characters from my youth, now confined to memory. I suppose they are never really gone while someone remembers them.

The last relics of the Bob Baxter epoch I can remember are Jerry (originally from Antrim) and Julie (originally) from Scotland, who magically breezed into my hometown of Bangor some time in the latter part of the 20th Century.

The photograph (overleaf, taken by my neighbour's son) depicts these two ghosts from a bye gone era at the top of Main Street in the town. They were both qualified teachers who, apparently had had enough of that life's format, preferring to wander about just as Bob Baxter did in the

1950's in Omagh.

Interestingly, this enduring image was taken the day the local town council banned consumption of alcohol in a public place; this is qualified by Jerry's lapel badge.

Out of view, however, are the open tin of Tennent's Extra in his hand and the bottle of Buckfast fine wine in Julies!

Maxima Memorias!!

Relative Normal Policing

"How far that little candle throws his beams"
The Merchant of Venice

Image: Publicity shot of myself on cycle patrol circa 1982, Strandtown Belfast. This shot was used as a PR exercise. Note Flackjacket and side arm.

Mediocrity has never been my bag; I knew this from before I left primary school. A "creeping common sense" never appealed to me, nor does it to this day. For example, year five, P5 as it was then called, found me seated between the teacher's desk and the chalk board at the front of the class for the whole duration of the year due, apparently, to me being disruptive. I felt like a church organist.

By contrast year seven, my final year before going to senior school and under a different teacher, I made pupil of the year. That Deputy Head Teacher, a giant of a man who wore his thinning red hair slicked back, looked taller that the chalk board and almost as wide from where I sat, wore a dark green woollen jacket with leather patches on the elbows and matching ribbons of leather around the cuffs. This was kind of uniform for all teachers in those days. He wore a white graph paper style shirt of a formal type button down with a teacher's tie, complimented with beige casual trousers, stay pressed they seemed. A traditional orange, aged with polish and multi-soled Patina's pattern brogues and who always smelt of, what I now know to be, Old Spice. He inspired me, for the first time in my life.

However, I digress. Upon completing my time in the special patrol group, I was allocated to Dundonald Police Station on the east of Belfast. Dundonald itself is an area poised as a gateway to and from Belfast on the extreme Eastern side of the city. Although the police station had been blown up by the provisional IRA in the early 70's it was then, I suppose, as close as you could describe as 'normal policing' in all my service past, present or future.

In common with all police stations it was surrounded by a 3m 'blast' bomb type wall crowned by that ubiquitous metal chicken wire. Entrance was gained by an electric operated gate overlooked by a security sanger occupied by a member of the police, complete with bullet proof glass and 24 hour security every day.

Identical in its structure to all other police stations built in the 1920's at the time Northern Ireland was partitioned from the rest of Ireland. It was basically 2 semi-detached houses, one half formally designed for the Station Sergeant and his family;

the other half was the Police Station proper.

All the station sergeants had long vacated this type of accommodation to live in either police constructed homes or private houses.

It had been given the nickname 'sleepy hollow' and although it comprised of two large, predominantly protestant council housing estates along with many privately owned homes, it was just that, a 'sleepy hollow'. Road traffic accidents, occasional assaults and domestic disputes were the order of the day. To be honest I was only there a short while when I wondered, "Where is the buzz?" This was a station best suited for officers commuting back and forward to surbia between duties, not for a young rooster like me. Nor the Sergeant in 'C' Section.

He was a veritable 'enigma wrapped in a riddle', we liked each other immediately. I can honestly say I learned more about police life and police ways from him, than any other person. Although I was not attached to his section, I would very much like to have been. Incidentally along with one of his female officers, later to become my girlfriend.

That aside, on overtime duties, or rest days, I sometimes worked with this man and invariably socialised with him after hours. He was always immaculate in appearance, probably then in his late 30's and standing not much over 5'8 but he had such presence, as they would say in racehorse circles. His round jolly face was topped with two steeply angled eyebrows and hawk eyes which stared unblinkingly. His head was topped by slightly thinning, dark hair tinged with, what looked like blue, which I suspect may have been tinted.

Although he spoke with a slight stutter, this man could sing like a bird, a reed warbler, or a black bird. He called me by my nickname and as he had a stutter, "CCCCCCCleeky". He was a rambler and a gambler and a long way from his home in Andersonstown in West Belfast where he had grown up as a schoolboy and his grandfather had served as a Sergeant in the post war years.

I was in awe of this man. He was indeed a gambler, finding solace in gambling on horses and cards and indeed many other manly pursuits. Although I knew he had connections and socialised in the company of "high rollers" such as Barney J Eastwood, the famous bookmaker at that time and being the Manager of the World Champion Boxer, Barry Maguigan from Clones. Although he knew them, he rarely spoke of them.

He once told me that after winning a famous boxing bout, Barry Maguigan declared on camera "I'd just like to thank my manager, Mr Eastwood, for teaching me all he knows". Mr Eastwood clarified this immediately with, no Barry, "I didn't teach you all I know, I taught you all you know".

If I had been working with his shift, afterwards invariably we would retire for refreshments to a local tavern. He educated me in many ways and often repeated his mantras of "Always keep your high hand low", or "Play your cards close to your chest", or "It's always better to travel first class, you meet a better class of crook".

I suppose out of all his favourites, the one I remember best and took advice from most was, "Be who you want to be CCCCCleeky, not what the world would like you to be. You're a ccccharacter, never let this old job change that. I'll tell you; it can take a lot more than it gives". I'd have to say my years of experience compounded this.

He was out on patrol one evening being driven by a Constable when they received a call reporting suspicious activity at the local chapel.

Albeit the area was predominantly protestant population, there was a small temporary chapel/portacabin at the bottom of the Dunlady Road with one door at its side. The only windows were small mesh covered openings near the roof. These were the only way to inspect the inside of the structure which was locked.

All seemed secured.

As the two officers were about to leave the scene, the stuttering Sergeant said to his driver, who was a burly officer, "Give me a llleg up to lllook inside and make sure I don't ffffucking fffall". This officer had played a lot of rugby in his days, so the Sergeant knew he was in safe hands. The Constable cupped his hands and Sergeant P climbed aboard. From his elevated vantage point and using his official issue or rubber ever ready torch to pierce the darkness, he glanced inside. Suddenly he seemed to lose his balance, so the Constable tightened his grip around the Sergeant's legs ensuring his safety. More shaking and stumbling ensued so the grip tightened. The Sergeant was safe and going nowhere, thought the Constable. Then, a lengthy stumbling and protracting command of "pppput mmmme down, it's a fffffuckin bbbbomb". Fortunately, it was only a hoax with an empty petrol tin and brightly coloured wires attached. This was verified by the Army Technical Officer who arrived later.

I didn't see him for a long time, this friend of mine. The last time I saw him he was on foot beat patrol, in the border town of Clogher in Co. Tyrone some fifty miles away. The year was 1982 or perhaps 1983. I had been promoted and was in an unmarked police car driving through the village. There he was resplendent in full uniform, immaculate as always. I couldn't believe it, he looked innocuous somehow. What? Why? What was he doing there? The plot unfolded.

In 1982, Alex "The Hurricane" Higgins, won the snooker championship for the second time. But that day, Sergeant P had been detailed to work as normal in Dundonald, where he remained after I had left, some two years prior to that. On that day, the famous Hurricane's opponent was bending down and considering a difficult shot in the final, one of the other cameras at the famous Crucible Theatre in Sheffield panned over to a pensive looking Higgins seated, clad in his usual open green shirt with white collar, black waistcoat and traditionally, no tie.

Directly behind him in the front row of the spectators sat an individual, clearly out of Dallas, or perhaps the Cannonball Run movie. Smartly dressed in crisp white linen jacket, matching Stetson hat and mirrored Ray Ban aviator style sunglasses sat, a supposedly, disguised Sergeant P. The story goes, he had not been granted annual leave the day of the final, although he had been presented with a special front row ticket by some of his associates to go along. Too good to miss, he decided to go on sick leave. Either he had been identified by some of his authorities, or someone else had 'touted' on him. The old disguise of Smokey and the Bandit had failed.

As a result of this breach of discipline, the authorities punished him via transfer to Clogher station some 60 miles away in rural Co. Tyrone.

I asked the driver to pull over and wound down the passenger window. I noticed almost immediately; he was wearing unmatching black footwear. We chatted for ages reminiscing and swapping tales. After some time, I received a radio call and had to leave. As we were parting I brought the issue of the non-matching footwear to his attention – made 'curiouser and curiouser' by the fact that one shoe was a casual lace up and the other a slip-on boot. I nonchalantly asked, "have you a sore foot Don". He threw his head back and burst out laughing, "No", he said. No explanation was given or asked for. "I suppose you have another pair just like that at home?" I asked. "Aagh Cccccleeky, you never lost it son".

AN ARMY OF ONE, 1983

The 'Grad'

I was never keen on the week of night shift once a month and tried to avoid it as much as possible. Of course, it had to be performed when working in a station where the duties demanded it – so I avoided these stations as much as I could.

Constable M (The Grad) was of the same disposition as me in Strandtown, but he simply didn't 'do' it! Named so because he obtained a degree in Astrophysics (or "Manchester United – The Evolution" of, or something).

Every 4th week 'The Grad' had a recurring ailment of something and got a line from his doctor for sick leave. He too, had passed the qualifying exam to Sergeant. On the day of the Promotion Board's which he and I attended, afterwards and in the police canteen I asked him how he got on. He replied in one word, which rhymes with kite! He elaborated, "Hardly had time for my arse to hit the chair", he shared. "Sick record Constable? – atrocious, come back in a year's time with the Inspectors' Exam passed and try again.

I don't think he ever did, nor was bothered. The 'job' never changed him; Sergeant P would have been proud.

Another time he had been too direct with his Sergeant in some matter, he was ordered out on beat patrol of the area. 'The Grad' was threatened with disciplinary action if he refused on his claim that foot patrol should only be conducted in pairs. I saw him later that day as he cut a lonesome figure strolling up the 4 x lane Newtownards Road in full overcoat, small (ladies) flack jacket and armed with an M1 Carbine. An army of one.

The Farce Side

"The time has come",
The walrus said,
"to talk of many things of shoes and ships and sealing wax of
cabbages and kings"
Lewis Carroll

In Solitude At Seaview

No3 SPG 1978

Every day was different in the SPG and in all my service generally. So, outside the 'Unit' (and we were precisely that; a 'Unit') pranks galore. For example, you couldn't go for a sit-down toilet in the 'bunker' without fear of being 'whooshed', i.e. a bucket of water thrown between the top of the toilet door and ceiling. Some brave souls in dire need did so under cover of their raincoats!

One episode occurred at a Christmas Section party in the bunker when 'The Cat' (then a C/Inspector IC) was whooshed by Const. S. He went home early muttering profanities as he skulked to his car. We never needed to secure our lockers, the only issue here was if it had been 'booby trapped' with a carton of water on opening. Stink bombs were another peril. Whilst driving home in your private car some colleague passes you making a gesture. Natural instinct, pedal to the metal and pursue. The soft crackling of a small glass phial of a stink bomb from under the pedal heralded disaster.

Seaview football ground on the Shore Road in Belfast was hosting the Co. Antrim Shield Cup soccer final. The entrance had already claimed the lives of both police officers and civilians in 'drive-by' shootings and was considered dangerous.

As usual the Cliftonville supporters were being flanked and escorted from primarily West Belfast, the New Lodge, the Antrim Road via Alexander Park Avenue and Skegoneill Avenue, the fans clad in bright red and white. Elevated and opposite the ground were playing fields surrounded by fencing. Constable E 13164 and I were detailed to enter through a gap in the fence, climb the raised area and 'keep an eye out' for any maverick supporters who may use this position to attack police below. We ascended with our little black issue Hemp kit bags containing the necessary equipment – Riot helmets, gloves, batons, (20 Benson & Hedges and lighter, Rennies (indigestion tabs etc etc)!

Everything was going fine; it was a beautiful summer evening. Unfortunately for us it was not raining.

As I cast my eye diagonally across the pitches to my horror, I noticed a file of red/white Cliftonville supporters gushing from 200m away through a hole in the fence. Constable E had been in my senior squad in the Training Centre, so he was the 'Senior man' and thus supposedly made our decisions. "Look, look", I shouted, "Fuck", he replied. No time to call for support or backup. There seemed to be 100's of them. Then to my horror they spied us. I thought of the films Zulu and Zulu Dawn about the British Army in South Africa in the Transvaal area – Zulu warriors of S.Africa and the slaughter of soldiers. I was not Michael Caine or Sergeant Chard and certainly no idiot!

He then uttered the immortal words "Do you want to stay together or spread out?"
"Spread out yourself or be spread out, I'm off", I replied. There was no time for an executive decision. I grabbed my kit bag, did a Jesse Owens and split back and down to the gap in the fence we had entered through. Strangely the only thing blocking my path at the exit was Constable E's ass.

"When danger reared its ugly head he bravely turned his tail and fled".

THE MAN FROM MAGHERA, BELFAST 1980

'He stumbled home from Clifden Fair with drunken song and cheeks aglow...."
James H Cousins

Northern Ireland is indeed a small dot on a world atlas situated to the North East of Ireland itself, which is a slightly larger dot. Its total inhabitants' amount to approximately 1.5 million or about the population of Rhode Island State in America. I am often fascinated by the number of strangers one meets there or indeed all over the world by chance who happen to know mutual acquaintances. Recently in a small part of South East Asia, I heard a slow and broad County Antrim lilt which belonged to Joe, a guy from Carnlough, 20 miles from my home, who knew my Aunt, 20 miles from him in Ballymena!

That aside: one evening whilst on mobile night duty patrol, I was following a Ford Escort car which was travelling along the main carriageway from Newtownards and towards Belfast. To digress for a moment, my father had owned a small business in the town of Newtownards supplying goods to all folks in the Ards Peninsula area which is very diverse and had been relatively unscathed by the troubles, everyone knowing each other and getting along fine. I used to work in his business. Once I had my driving license as a treat and after work, I had to drive him and his cronies around the area in search of Beer And Refreshments (BAR) in his old Ford Granada which had once been pride of some fleet.

At the tip of the beautiful Newtownards Peninsula and the confines of Strangford Lough which is an area of natural beauty because of its marine life, flora and fauna lies the picturesque village of Portaferry. A short car ferry to the equally beautiful village of Strangford and all of its surrounding areas which have been used many times for film locations and in particular the extremely popular "Game of Thrones".

It was from a tiny bar in Portaferry it transpired the driver of this Escort has been coming from in the early hours of the morning following a traditional Fleadh Coel (music festival) where he had obviously been enjoying himself socially and in his capacity as a fiddle player. I knew this little bar very well as I had often been in it drinking Coca Cola whilst my father and his associates made merriment over the evening.

Indeed, it was there I heard for the first time a traditional Irish ballad which I was to hear many times over the coming years (and particularly in County Fermanagh) called 'Sean South from Garryowen'.

I eventually managed to have the vehicle stopped at the side of the road opposite the Ulster Hospital. The driver was on his own and when I opened the car door to ask for his driving documents, he seemed to lose his balance somewhat and spilled onto the tarmac landing on his shoulder. I assisted him in manoeuvring himself out of the vehicle and onto his feet. I should add that 'his eyes were heavily glazed; his speech was slurred, and he was unsteady on his feet' the usual police jargon at that time for describing one incapable of driving. To put it mildly this gent was somewhat 'blootered!' How he had made the 20-mile journey from Portaferry to Newtownards via the coastal route and not ended up in the sea in itself was a considerable feat.

This was a decent wee country man who was intending to make his way home to the south Derry village of Maghera in the County of Londonderry. I knew this village well as the previous year I had ended up being pushed through a hedge on its outskirts by an unruly mob we were escorting on foot from Toomebridge in Co Antrim through Maghera to Dungiven and thence to Burntollet Bridge upon the 10th year commemoration of a Civil Rights march from January 1969. This would have been an arduous enough drive, even at daytime and in sobriety!

I removed the car keys from the ignition and locked the vehicle. I took pity on this old gent and decided not to arrest him for being Drunk in Charge due to me knowing the publican who plied him with copious amounts of alcohol over the day(s)! He shook my hand and thanked me profusely. He then asked where he might go? I looked across to the Ulster Hospital and the warmth of the 24-hour casualty waiting area. Though sparse in furnishings, it would be adequate for him to sober up. I then escorted him across the 4 lanes of carriageway, fearing he may be knocked down, then on to the casualty entrance.

When we parted company, I told him to pick the keys up in Dundonald Police Station Enquiry Office a short distance away but not before 9.00am. Again, he thanked me and asked my name. I declined to give him it but told him my number was '999'!

DMSU FERMANAGH 1980 - 1981

'Film night, not tonight, darling'
Luan Peters, Artistic Film Actor

Occasionally at the end of a long shift finishing in the early hours of the morning some of the residents in the portacabins of our camp would retire to the recreation area to relax with a beer or two. Sometimes Herbie in our crew would produce some alternative adult viewing to compliment the refreshments.

On these occasions the lights were dimmed and there were normally 3 rows of those large lounging chairs placed in a semi-circle. In this seedy smoke-filled atmosphere, the assembled viewers would lounge with their ties off, boots placed to the back of the seat in front, beer in hand anxiously waiting for the show to commence.

From the 3rd row I could see various heads and scalps with a plethora of scalps and hair styles on display and silhouetted by the flickering images to their front – bushy or side parted, flat top or wispy, some devoid of thread, these seen turning this way and that, imparting observations and comic asides or ideas.

The mutterings were occasionally interrupted by 'clink – pshh' as another can was opened. Whisperings in low breathless tones to one another. Savoury remarks such as 'Wowar!' or "Naaa average I'd say", 'Get on with it' or 'Must be a good book' etc etc etc.

The entire setting was reminiscent of a – 'Film – noir' premier complete with critics seated cosily.

I remember one scene vividly; it showed a curvaceous and scantily clad woman of undetermined vintage. It seemed she was just about to go to, or had just got up from, bed. She was poised on the side of a large bed complete with canopy which looked well capable of accommodating King Henry VIII with all of his 6 wives.

Image: Film Night, Enniskillen circa 1980

Adorning the table by its side was a small tiffany lamp and a cream and pink 70's style telephone with the disk dial on front. She spun the large numbered disk on the front a number of times, she placed the hand piece to her left ear with her left hand, left elbow resting on her crossed nylon clad knee and just in front of her ample bosom, she was studying the brightly coloured fingernails of her right hand waiting for the line to connect. Our room was deadly silent.

Suddenly the tranquillity was abruptly disturbed by the piercing bell clanging of our own recreational room phone.

A wit immediately sprang up from the gloom of the front stalls and shouted "That'll be for me!"

BELFAST STRANDTOWN 1982

'The Unknown Stuntman'
'A friend should bear his friends infirmities'
William Shakespeare - Julius Ceasar (Act 4, Scene 3)

I had learned to ride motorcycles when I was about 12 on the waste ground outside my hometown 'the lead mines'. It was a vast area of hill, rocks and fields above and behind the local public amenity site and perfect for learning. All types and shapes of motorcycles were seen from Honda 90's with mud guards removed for that moto/cross look, Montesa, Bultaco, Ossa, early Yamahas all carrying riders of various levels of ability.

I then progressed onto road bikes and many a happy hour was spent on the pier which we called 'The Paddock' beside the McKee clock in Bangor. These were a great bunch of mostly young men with whom I became very friendly. The craic was 90!

Because of these happy memories I, of course, had (and have) a soft spot for these kindred spirits to this day. One evening we were performing a vehicle check point (VCP) on the North Road in Belfast at a junction with Cyprus Avenue. There were 6 or 7 of us, 2 men with rifles at either end of the road stop protecting the other members talking to drivers and requesting documents. I saw a motorbike on the approach, and it was not possible to turn away because of the positioning of the VCP. I spoke to its rider, a youth probably 18 or 19 and as usual asked for his licence and insurance. He showed me his licence which was in order and told me his insurance certificate was back in his house a short distance away. This was long before central records were held on a central computer base. For some reason I suspected he didn't have any. I looked him straight in the eye and said, "You don't have any do you?", he paused, lowered his eyes and said, "No". I thought for a moment and then decided not to report him. I couldn't put him down for a formal caution as it was too serious of a motoring offence. After a moment I told him that if I stopped him again, I would report him. He looked up at me shocked through his full-face helmet and said, "Are you not going to report me then?" "No, not as long as you pull a wheelie when you move off", I replied "I'll report you if you don't". He looked around him and selected first gear and moved just around the corner. When out of view of all officers he dipped the clutch, revved the engine and in front headlight rose up like a python and shone high into the branches of the conifers above. He then disappeared from view, just like the Lone Ranger. "Did anyone get his number some shocked officer cried?", "Na, too quick", I replied.

Fast forward to 1984 and the Friday evening before the North West 200 road race at Portrush, Co Antrim, Northern Ireland around 60 miles from Belfast. Four of us had travelled up in a Ford Escort van and were staying in Portstewart that evening in order to watch the races the next day. We had split up and I was in a large hotel with a disco, where I had met a charming young lady. She was keen to watch the moonlight dancing on the waves with the beach strand in front and in the comfort of my pal's red van. Everything was very romantic until the time came to leave the beach. The van had sunk to is axle in the sand and would not move. I noticed the tide was approaching. King Canute had failed in his efforts, so my only option was to return to the hotel and the music and ask for assistance.

The reader should appreciate that in those days it was not ideal to be recognised as a member of any security force off duty. However, I felt safe enough in my old worn leather biker's jacket, jeans, boots and unshaven look, complete with longer hair. As I was working in Rosslea border Police/Army base, it was permitted to wear your hair longer.

I entered the dance hall where everything was in full swing. The first group of men with their backs to me looked fit enough to help push the van free. I tapped a big 6-footer on the shoulder and told him my problem. Another 3 or 4 heads turned around to look at me. When he spoke, I almost soiled my pants. "You're a cop aren't you fella?" "No, I'm a fireman", I replied. "Na, definitely a cop, I know you". I tried to swiftly plan my retreat.

"You stopped me in Belfast one night and told me to do a wheelie". I was shocked. And stunned.

He turned to his team and said, "This one's ok, he let me off with no insurance", and held out his right hand. What a relief. We all walked down to the Strand and we helped my maiden and I. It just goes to show; you reap what you sow.

We remain friends to this day.

Image: 'On the Wheel' Donaghadee, 1977

STRANDTOWN, BELFAST 1982 - THE STING

'I have never been in a situation so dismal, that a policeman couldn't make it worse'
Anon

Whilst working in Strandtown Police Station every member was kept busy in a wide and varied selection of reportable police incidents. I suppose one of the less popular were fatal traffic accidents or other sudden deaths. I certainly did not relish the thought of being the first on the scene of a dead body. However, I was not alone. Other than traffic accidents sudden deaths occurred frequently in the winter months when the weather was colder, or some older poor folk had succumbed to hypothermia.

And so, it was one bright November morning when the crisp frost refused to abate all day. Big Kenny was my mate. Although slightly junior to me in service we had arrived in the Police Station one day apart. We were both tall with the same stature and the same sense of humour and initially mistaken for one another. When Kenny and another young Constable Stanley and I were out together on patrol the shift flew by. The morning in question, I was observer in the primary patrol vehicle and as such it was my duty to attend to all necessary paperwork. Kenny was the 'extra observer' sitting in the rear armed with a machine gun in case of attack and the driver was a female officer. Around 10.30 that morning we were just about to return out on patrol after our tea break when the telephonist in the station asked to speak to me as I was dealing with all calls. She told me that a neighbour had requested the milkman to gain entrance to her adjoining house via an open rear window as the single elderly lady occupant had not been seen for some days. He had done so and discovered her lying dead in one of the upstairs bedrooms. I grabbed the other two members and off we went.

The house was only 3 minutes away from our base, but the telephonist had confirmed that this call was genuine. This was normal practice to ensure the call was not a hoax to lure security force personnel into a possible ambush.

Whilst on route, Ken asked me whereabouts the remains of the person were in the house? He seemed a little cocky and glad not to be first on the scene. Without hesitation, flinching or looking around at him I casually informed him that the remains of the dear old lady were lying in a back kitchen and downstairs. He accepted this.

When we arrived the front door to the semi-detached house was open. The driver remained with the vehicle as usual; both Kenny and I approached the hallway. The narrow, carpeted stairs appeared on the left and rose upwards and out of sight disappearing around a return landing.

I nonchalantly asked my colleague if 'he would take a wee peek upstairs' as I strolled down the hallway in the direction of the downstairs kitchen and pantry. I glanced to the left and saw his legs disappear out of view. I stopped and simply waited glancing upwards, whilst out of his sight.

I heard his nervous tuneless whistle receding into a room. The click of his boots indicated that would be the bathroom. The whistle got slightly louder and then I heard the noise of the bottom of the door on carpet as it opened inwards to a bedroom. Pause, whistling continued as he emerged. Two down 2 to go I thought, the tension and my excitement mounted. Then the creek of the 3rd door interrupted suddenly by the sharp intake of breath and a muffled yell

"Willie!", he shouted whilst he bounded 3 gigantic strides down the stairs, his forage hat dislodged and falling behind him with his left hand on the newel post at the bottom of the stairs he skidded to his knees whilst trying to negotiate a 180 degree turn towards me. His eyes were hollows of madness as he cried out "There's another one up there in the bedroom!!" "Really?", I enquired nonchalantly, I couldn't hold back any longer. He questioned my parentage, shook his head and stormed out of the house.

KINCORA BOYS HOME, BELFAST 1982

The Sound of Silence
Simon & Garfunkle

Kincora Boys' Home in East Belfast caused a lot of controversy due to alleged incidents which occurred (or did not) in the 60's and 70's. In much the same way the Catholic Church has received adverse press more recently the home had been vacated and closed pending enquiries and now only housed a caretaker.

It was our area on one crisp spring morning we received a call to a burglary there. As I drove Constable M to the scene, the radio crackled with unapproved transmissions from anonymous wits all on channel 5 about this.

An authoritative warning from the controller curtailed the radio traffic. For a while at least, the RUC Code of Conduct was not always strictly adhered to on the police radio networks, indeed on some occasions the ability to overhear other terminals was sometimes cut off and a series of beeps letting others know another station was transmitting. Only the experienced voice of the HQ Controller was to be heard then.

Anyhow, the procedure after receipt of a call was to announce the result of the said burglary to HQ in the standard format of how, where, when the culprits had gained admission to the scene.

The ex-Teacher turned Police Constable M was the observer attending the call in my car. He was a lovely gent about 6-7 years my senior who had informed me that, although he had been a qualified teacher for a while, he had always wanted to be a policeman.

He realised his ambition in the early 1980's and was excellent at his job. I never saw him in a panic, his elocution educated voice always pitch perfect, annunciation a joy to hear and grammatically faultless.

We arrived at the scene. I knew the call result would be needed but remained solemn.

He alighted from the police car, resplendent as usual, cap proudly perched, clipboard and pen as always by his side and disappeared through a large green Georgian fanned front door to consult the caretaker.

A short while later he emerged. I watched him as he approached along the path between the lawns to the police car. My heart pounded as he sat down in the passenger seat, lifted the radio microphone. Time stopped. In a plummy matter of fact BBC broadcaster's voice he calmly and clearly broke the silence. "Uniform from Echo Tango 70" official mature voice from HQ "70 send over" "Reference this burglary call to Kincora Boys' Home, entry gained to the rear sometime during the night".

No response from HQ, a long and protracted silence, Constable M looked at me inquiringly and asked innocently, "Do you think he received that result?" Talk through was off – just constant beep – beep – beep

I corpsed – couldn't draw breath.

For the first time I can remember, the communications controller was speechless!

Image: Kincora Boys Home, Belfast 1982

CARRICKMORE RUC STATION 1985

'Indiscretion is the better part of valour'
'Elementary, my dear Watson'
Sir A.C. Doyle

In the mid 1980's I was a Station Sergeant at Carrickmore RUC Station in Mid-Ulster, East Tyrone. A foot patrol had been out in the early hours of the morning and stopped a woman in a car along the Drumnakilley Road. We knew that she didn't work, and she didn't smoke. She was actually in charge of the Cumānn-ńa-mban Woman's Division of the IRA. They stopped her, searched her and questioned her as to what she was doing out in the early hours of the morning. They found numerous bits and pieces of interest along with various documents in her vehicle.

"In her car they seized a pack of sandwiches, a flask and address book, a pack of 20 cigarettes, one lighter, one camera, and last but not least, a tub of Flora margarine".

These items were seized under emergency legislation and the reason being the address book could have been suspicious enough, carrying maybe information about members of security forces on or off duty, as could the camera. Bearing in mind, she didn't smoke or work and because of the flask and sandwiches, the boys thought that maybe she was heading to a couple of fellow terrorists lying up in the hills, maybe sitting at the end of a bell push, or a bomb for a security patrol passing. Anyway, they seized the contents of the vehicle and arrived back into the station with it and told me what had happened. I told them to record what they had seized in the special property register and I also said "photocopy the contents of the address book and take the film out of the camera in case there in anything really worth looking at".

Really what we should have done was hold it for a day or two and then give it back. They asked how long we should hold it. I replied, "The only problem I can see here are the sandwiches", because obviously they were perishable.

Next day, Fergie was upstairs doing the phones and from my office (which was down below), I heard the phone ringing. He buzzed down and he said, "Danny Morrison", who was the Sein Fein MP for Mid-Ulster at that time, "is on the phone, he wants to speak to the Station Sergeant". Well, I was kind of stuck as the Inspector was off. I had no choice, I told him to put him through to me. I knew rightly the boys in the station were listening because you could hear the echo on the line. Danny Morrison asked who he was speaking to and I told him. He introduced himself and said, "I'll tell you what it is Sergeant, one of my constituents", bla bla bla. I knew exactly what was coming and I knew what the problem was going to be. He carried on, "was stopped yesterday morning, are you aware of the incident". I responded that I was, and he continued, "well, the problem is that she had several items seized under emergency legislation, can you tell me exactly what is going to happen to these items". I tried to deflect by saying, "well, they will be returned in due course". But I knew what was coming. Then the sixty-four-million-dollar question was, "what about the sandwiches, because they are perishable".

It is quoted here in a copy of Án Phoblac (Republican News), which I received all the way from Philadelphia, addressed to RUC Clegg, Sergeant North of Ireland, it states about the items being seized and then mentioned, "when challenged the next day for the return of the items, including the sandwiches as they are perishable, RUC Sergeant Clegg mirthfully declared, "sure if they are hard, she can always toast them".

VEHICLE CHECK POINT, FINAGHY ROAD NORTH

No3 SPG Belfast 1978 - A Special Delivery

There was another occasion when I was in a special patrol group in Belfast, it was a Sunday morning. We didn't often work Sundays, one in six maybe. The city was quiet, and we were doing a vehicle check point up at the bridge at Finaghy Road North, leading towards Andersonstown on the Lisburn Road in Belfast. We had set up the check point and I was at the top of the bridge with a rifle, providing cover towards the direction of Andersonstown. We had been there for maybe fifteen or twenty minutes, maybe even twenty-five and I was getting a bit bored to be honest. Next thing, I saw this fella coming walking up the road towards us and I thought I'd stop him, pass the time and maybe strike up a conversation. I said, "how are you". I did the usual procedure, where are you coming from, where are you going etc. He said he was coming from the Lisburn Road, I said, "Oh, where do you live?", he said he lived up in Owenvarragh Park, which was in Andersonstown, quite a distance away. I'm wondering what he was doing on the Lisburn Road, so I said, "are you just out for a dander then," says I, "it's Sunday morning". He said, "aye, aye". I said, "just turn out your pockets there so I can see what you've got". I just felt there was something, not right, about him, he looked…. edgy.

Next thing, I opened his coat and inside there were all these letters and post, pamphlets. It wasn't from his house in Owenvarragh Park they were addressed to, it was where he had been coming from, some house off the Lisburn Road. I said, "what are you doing with all this post?", "Awe", he said, "the postman delivered to our house yesterday by mistake. I was just down there to put it in the proper house, but there was nobody there, so I'm gonna call back". I couldn't believe what I was hearing, I said, "Do you think I'm fuckin stupid". I took him down to the Sergeant and I said, "this guy here is a part-time mail man it seems".

We wrapped up the check point, confirmed the address and we all hopped into the land rover with this guy in the back. We went around to the house where the post was from, sure enough, the back door was lying open, he had burgled the place. Been caught red handed. So, we headed down, he was arrested, and we headed down to the Lisburn Road Police Station in Belfast to get the local detectives to sort it out. So, on the way down he says, "what do you think will happen to me?". I said, "well, depends on a few things, have you any previous form or convictions?"

"Aye, a wee bit of previous but it was a couple of years ago". I said, "aye, you'll likely get charged with burglary and if it's your first offence with burglary you might get lucky enough and maybe get off with a suspended sentence. If the judge is in the right mood and your previous form isn't too bad". So, he said, "what, is that it, nothing else?", "well", I said, "you're obviously gonna get a fine as well". He looked quite indignant and said, "well, how am I gonna pay a fine". So, joking with him, I said, "well, don't worry they will accept cheques", so he says, "I've got no money", I said, "are you not working at all son", he said, "no", I said, "did you ever think of joining the police?" with a serious face he said, "do you wanna get me fuckin shot".

I kept my face straight.

DROWNING, ROSSLEA

A WINTER'S TALE
Shakespeare

Then there was another incident in Roslea where, if he wasn't an IRA activist, he was certainly a sympathiser and he had been arrested a couple of times and taken in for questioning. Anyway, he had been out fishing on a lake nearby and unfortunately, he had couped off the boat and fallen into the lake and drowned. The police were called to the scene and the body was taken away. Then, obviously the job was to inform the next of kin who was his wife who lived in the Roslea area.

So a pal of mine knocked the door and the next thing the door opened, he hadn't opened his mouth and this wife, this fishwife started giving a tirade of abuse about, "ya bastards", and this and that the other, "yis are never done, you're never away from this door," and "leave him alone, yis have had him in that Armagh and beaten him up and "I hope they blow youse all up, bastards, the lot of youse". "Get away, fuck off" and this and that, giving an awful tirade of abuse. So, when she paused for breath, my pal said, "ah, does the widow Murphy live here".

SELF CATERING & RADIO RECIPES

'I cook with wine, sometimes I even add it to the food'
W.C. Fields

Having served in several border posts during my earlier career and latter career in the Royal Ulster Constabulary (George Cross), all single men have to learn basic cooking skills, as in those years there were no canteens. Well; there was a canteen in the police bar, but it wasn't in any way, manned by professional chefs or canteen staff, as they would be nowadays. So, being ferried in and out by army helicopter for duties of four to seven days, sometimes more due to adverse weather conditions, or the exigencies of duty. Provisions were either brought in at the commencement of the shift or cadged from the army cooks present. Normally these were joint army/police, barracks or police stations.

Most of the junior officers learned and took their turn at cooking a chicken on Sundays whilst the rest of the guys were out on foot patrols. Sunday lunch being ready upon their return. One lesson was normally given to a junior member by someone who knew what they were doing; it was expected then that the junior member would be able to, in due course, cook a turkey or a chicken on his own or whatever meal he decided to cook for a Sunday.

Although I never mastered the art of bakery, I became an adequate cook. One recipe will always be in the oven of my mind. One morning while I was on the early shift (0700 – 1500) in Belfast, our crew was availing of the morning tea break, as was the custom. Regularly on a local Belfast radio station at around 1030, a person would telephone in live a short recipe to the female broadcaster who was called Candy

Divine.

Our station was always tuned into this same radio station, as the station cleaner who also doubled up as the cook, or bun maker or toast maker, toasted scones etc, listened religiously to this channel.

At that time, the low tech transmitting station did not have, what they have now called, the ten second integrity tape whereby a conversation, although it was live it would be delayed for five to ten seconds to enable any improprieties to be edited out prior to going on the air. In those days, this radio station didn't seem to have it. Either that or it was simply not in operation on that day. Anyway, the conversation went something like this,

Candy Divine (Local Radio Station)
"That was 'How Deep is your Love' by the Bee Gees. So good morning caller, who do we have on the line this morning?"
Joe Smith (Caller)
"Morning Candy, this is Joe Smith"
Candy Divine
"So what local recipe do you have for us today Joe?"
Joe Smith
"It's a recipe I found, written by my dear old granny in a little book my wife found in the attic recently called 'Dingleberry Pie"
Candy Divine
"Ooh sounds wonderful. So how did you make this special pie?"
There now followed a lengthy recipe shared by Joe, presumably read from this recently found treasure of a recipe book. It included the making of the pastry, amounts of various ingredients, oven temperature, times as would be expected. His narrative, very informative.

Candy Divine
"Emmmm Joe, sounds delicious, so tell me and the listeners, where does your granny find her dingleberries Joe?"
Joe Smith
"Pluck them off yer ass Candy"

Quiet, indefinite, radio silence followed.

LORD, WHAT FOOLS THESE MORTALS BE

'LORD, WHAT FOOLS THESE MORTALS BE'
Shakespeare - A Midsummer Night's Dream (Act 3, Scene 2, Line 115)

Or "No bird soars too high, if it soars with its own wings"
Or "even a hawk is an eagle amongst crows"
Or "Their finest hour"
Or "In flagrante delicto"
Or Who??!!

My favourite all time insult was delivered whilst I stood on duty at a public demonstration in Derry / Londonderry as a Sergeant when someone announced to me;

"Shit flies high when it gets hit with a stick Hey!!"

Who?...... Was the Superintendent who, when advising one of his Constables whose home was under a terrorist threat of attack suggested as a solution, "Get some Geese Constable, the Romans used them you know, make great guard dogs. Only downside is they shit everywhere".

Who?...... Was the well-known charismatic Senior Officer in charge of a large body of officers in Belfast when once attended a large and formal regimental dinner representing the police as a guest; The regimental silver was brought out, each person present having a non-commissioned officer attending him. Seven courses followed, then a toast to the Queen, cigars lit, and Port passed to the left in long term honoured fashion. When asked by his 'Butler' if he would require anything else? The Superintendent replied, "I like to finish a big feed with some bread and jam".

Who?......Was the Chief Inspector who lost his cool when a member was asked to sign the Divisional Caution Book for the alleged offence of 'Bringing the force into disrepute' whilst off duty and refused to do so? When hustled further and asked, 'what could possibly be the problem', the Sergeant concerned suggested the Chief Inspector to "Sign it yourself and mark it as refused to sign".

Who?......Was the Senior Officer when asked the possible outcome of an event replied that, it really didn't matter as it was all "Swings and rowing boats".

Who?......Was the Weapon Training Branch Inspector that stated:
"Spring is a wonderful time of year, what with the birds singing and the bees 'polluting' the flowers".

Who?...... Was the, well known, 'Poacher- turned- gamekeeper' who proudly declared that the formal Christmas dinner would include, "Ten-inch steaks and PaBaloBa!!".

Who?...... Was the Valium laden Chief Inspector who hung up his landline phone during an extended rant to a Sergeant over a minor misdemeanour? When the Sergeant suggested that, as he was under the table in his office with 2 other men with mortars landing, "There was probably more appropriate time to discuss this".

Who?...... Was the dapper young detective I spied gracing the corner of a bar in Holywood dressed in a grey woollen 3-piece Dougie Hayward bespoke suit complete with Barker brogues and hanging off the end of a gold tipped Balkan Sobrini imported Cheroot? Only my old colleague from the late 70's in the Fermanagh/ Tyrone border who had come up trumps! Well done Paulsie.

Who?...... Was the well-known Lay Visitor who in the early hours of one morning upon descending to a rural Custody Suite suggested to a detained prisoner that they may have cause for complaint against the Duty Custody Sergeant. She left swiftly when the prisoner asked the same Custody Sergeant to note a formal complaint about "That 'aul' bag for waking me up".

Who?...... Was the Superintendent formally named by all as 'Lusard' (Police Academy films)? when he urged one of his Constables to 'seek mental treatment'. The Constable then asked of the Superintendent what formal qualifications he held to suggest such assistance? When the Superintendent replied, "None", the Constable then politely suggested that the same treatment be sought by the Superintendent.

Who?...... Was the well-known Senior Constable, when referred to as 'Mad' and 'Out of control' proudly produced and brandished a formal certificate affirming his sanity!? (RIP 'The Erk').

Who?...... Was the Senior Officer required to resign following a complaint by a member of the public that the off-duty Policeman was 'prancing around' the (well-known park in Lisburn, County Antrim) in a long wig, Laura Ashley type dress and high heels soliciting passers-by?'

Who?...... Was the newly promoted Senior Officer who was only (thankfully) temporarily attached to a 'Special Category' County Tyrone Police Station. Upon the partial explosion of a 200lb booby-trap explosion on a Police Foot Patrol leaving their base, (causing two officers to be covered in unexploded substances), he claimed to me that the IRA bomb incident was "only staged to scare us"!!

Lord help us all!

And finally, 'Park Ranger' (Sl. Stranger)

Who?...... Was the retired officer who met his also retired Superintendent in a Police Rehabilitation Centre in 2004? When the Officer was asked by the Superintendent what had happened to his blonde and highlighted hair the officer replied that he was now "Living in Spain".

The Cat replied, "I always knew you had been out in the sun too long Willie!!"

Image: Outside Red Section in Musgrave Street, 1986

Fate, Destiny, Karma

Instinct is a wonderful thing
William Clegg 13219

'There are more things in heaven and earth, Horatio, than are dreamt of in your philosophy'

INSTINCT (Instingkt) n, an involuntary or unreasoning prompting to action; the natural impulse by which animals are guided, apparently independent of reason, or experience to any action; intuition. (The Modern Illustrated Home Dictionary 1935)

On a golden summers' day in July 1965 the sun directly overhead shone and sparkled on every crest of the North Atlantic Ocean whilst it waved as far as the eye could see westward towards the horizon and the East Coast of America.

The sand coloured ford corsair carrying five occupants breezed its way over the Davitt Bridge; the geographical artery supplying a lifeline to Achill Island in County Mayo, Ireland from Newport on the Mainland.

The yell of fear and screech of brakes veered, the vehicle abruptly and unceremoniously towards its right-hand side and certain tragedy over the verge and into the frothing foamy waters over '30' feet below. We stopped inches from doom. 'Todavía no señor', the moment lasted an eternity.

When my father spun around to his left in the driver's seat, his sunglasses were displaced, the right leg almost on top of his head, curiously revealing one piercing, dilated bovine eye which seemed to look through me as I remained cast in the centre of the rear seat. "Everyone OK?!" he asked. Silence. Oddly I could hear cries of dismay in the distance.

Then I saw them, also, a small group of people had congregated around a young man who had fallen to the road from the canopy of a coniferous bush which spanned wind swept overhead most of the road. He was exactly where we would have driven had my father not swerved violently. Fortunately, he was uninjured.

Later that day from our Keel guest house my father tried to explain that 'instinct' could not be explained by medicine or science but was in everyone with various measures, was there to protect us, should never be ignored and always to be acted upon.

I imagine, to a 7-year-old, it must have sounded as easy to comprehend as a quadratic equation: nevertheless, I always remembered his advice throughout my life.

Some 30 years later during an idyllic early summer evening I was reminiscing to myself about some of those impactive events that had occurred whilst serving in the Royal Ulster Constabulary.

Also acutely aware that there were others where my ignorance was bliss, I found myself having walked several miles along the banks of the Lower Bann river as it languished and methodically meandered relentlessly to the setting west and the road bridge which demarcates the village of Portglenone to the Counties of Antrim and Londonderry.

In an explosive micro-second I sensed it. I turned to my right on instinct just as an ebullient electric blue streak darted low along the length of the wide river, its tiny wing tips tickling the surface. In my minds eye I can still see the conflicting bright amber on the chest making an innocuous and stunning contrast to its predominantly translucent turquoise blue head and wings. In an instant, this enchanting and enigmatic creature had vanished amongst a cacophony of birds, dragonflies and insects all calling it a day above the surface.

I had never seen a kingfisher before, or since, nor needed to. I imagine many unfortunate souls never do....

Now in my 60's, I see this golden moment as something more, perhaps even a metaphor for life?

EPILOGUE

CONCLUSION

It's summer now, the consequence being that my Autumn years approach. I'm sitting in a diner with my ten-year-old son, Will. The conclusion to my wee paper has taken almost as long as the rest.

My son just asked me what I was thinking about? I explained my dilemma. Quick as a flash he answered, "Maybe your brain is enjoying the writing so much that it won't let you think of how to finish it"

Eureka! So that's how I'll conclude, after all ....

The Past is never dead,
it's not even past ......

Thanks to:-

Doctors, Nurses, Operational Health Unit,
Convalescence Homes, Support Staff and
all those people who treated and assisted
Police Officers throughout the world whilst
Injured in the line of duty.

Our Eternal Thanks

(Oh, and to the Roman and Greek Gods Bacchus & Dionysus)

ROLL OF HONOUR

Where are they now?
Nicknames awarded in the Line of Duty

ROLL OF HONOUR

Nicknames awarded in the line of duty

Whether they knew it or not, everyone earned or was appointed with a nickname, which was always relevant to some (mis)deed, habit, appearance, preference or opinion they may have had. Here are some I remember vividly. Their real names have not been included for obvious reasons.

You know who you are!!

Smokey Joe
Cosmo
Barney Rubble
Jilted John
Freda
The Reverend
Happy Days
Powder Monkey
Joker
Pyscho
Scobey
Brains
Wobble Neck
Shoulder Length Parting
Hoaker
Hoagie
Dr. Death

Lenny
Gentleman John
Myself-In-The-Hot Spur
Jiffy
Gunga-Din
Sniper's Nightmare
Greasy Fwy
Bomber
Mad Dog
Pretty Boy
Smokey Bacon
Baaaaaa!
Sid Snot
Valium Villie
Alfie Tupper
Roger Ramjet
Prince of Darkness

Hangman's Nightmare
Liberty Valance
Steeky
Betty
B.A
Cruncher
Rugs
Shammy
Windy
Skull Dogs
Penis
Grizzly Adams
K.B
Victor Alpha is 2
Wreckless Eric
Joey
Bo-Bo
The Half 'un
Lurch
Hole-In-The-Head
Bobby Charlton
Bamber
The Nine Stone Cowboy
Dim-But-Nice
Black Dart
Weebley
TTHHHKIPPER
Buck
Trendy Brendy
Rupert
Spin-Us-A-Yarn
Take a powder
Big Red
Mountain Man
Quiet Man
Will-You-Do-The-Five

Max Headroom
Mutiny
Pedro
Slim-Boy-Fat
Dipstick
Joe-Last-Fag
The Greek
Tank
I.Copious
Heck
Sidney
Hustle
Galdirt
Harpic
Cosey Powell
Huck
Crap-In-The-Hat
Wingnut
Bunter
The Griff
Jupe
The ToJo
D.D
Hulk
De Wig
Glorey Hole
Limpey
Jupiter Head
Big Dish Northy
Big Bad Bob
The Blah
Murt-Murtah
Purvie
Big Biggs Nobby
Whistler
Two Pounds

Fletch
Wilbar
Dibble
The Big Lad
Chestnut Mare
Straw
Poser
I'll Stop That
Jockey
Binman's Helper
Loco
Flash
The Sheriff
Rooster
Clitman
Legend
The King
Dixie
Goofy
Big Dave
Big Ma
Max
Toot-toot
Eusabio
Roy Rodgers
Space Invader Head
Griff
Specky
Lunn
Delbar
Rapid Roy
Big Jim Slade
Sooty Roberts
Hawarence
Kit
Jooles

Spill-The-Drink
Carter (The Farter)
Hunt
Dead Eyes
Badger
Pete Pistola
Sniffer
Pubic Head
Narco-Lo
Big Bert
Blondie
Harry-Harold
Coynah
Mackers
Dosser
Chipper
Bounder
Joey The Kid
Wartie
Wing Nut
The Plant
Gandi
The Plank
Nought-And-Carry-One
Gupta
Big Da
Killer
The Wako Kid
Stretch
Drewser
Pole Vaulter
Betty
Peterson
Sparky
Alfie Tupper
Big Pete

Smiling Assassin
Daisey
Croop
Drallab Einnor
Dawser
Mackers
Roger D'Eclare
Bo-Bo
Big Ted
Rugs
K.B.
Big Ray
Malcolm
Bongo

Gilo
Smiler
Colonel 'H'
'M'
Sebastian
Big J.R.
Thompo
Flower
Hushie
B.T.O.
Scallion Head
Kenny Baby
Yogi Bear
Colgate

And a special mention to my friend Paul 'Gunner' Graham (Detective 12662).

ACKNOWLEDGEMENTS

The family of Ex. Supt. R Buchanan (RIP)

-o0o-

The Historical Society

-o0o-

Mr 'Pop' Alexander, Vice Head Teacher
at Ballyholme Primary School, Bangor, Co Down
(Year 7)

-o0o-

Sandra Parry of SP Solutions Bangor

-o0o-

Tina, and the team at
Excalibur Press, Belfast

-o0o-

Pacemaker Press, Belfast

ABOUT THE AUTHOR

William John Terence Clegg is single, identifies as male and lives in Indonesia.

Upon leaving school at 18, he trained briefly in underwater construction before entering Enniskillen Royal Ulster Constabulary Training Depot as a recruit in March 1978.

William regards himself as privileged to have worked in and survived the challenges inherent in high risk, hostile, urban and rural environments throughout the province of Northern Ireland together with training department, where his influences are still felt and resonate to this very day.

He was born in Co Down and returns frequently to spend time with his son. William also occupies himself with scuba diving, motorcycling, reading and enjoying memories with those survivors who can still remember!

"My old friend Ben"